The Eternal Venture Spirit
An Executive's Practical Philosophy

The Eternal Venture Spirit
An Executive's Practical Philosophy

Kazuma Tateisi
Founder and Former Chairman
Omron Tateisi Electronics Co.

Productivity Press
CAMBRIDGE, MASSACHUSETTS
NORWALK, CONNECTICUT

Productivity Press   Productivity, Inc.
P.O. Box 3007   or   101 Merritt 7 Corporate Park
Cambridge, MA 02140   Norwalk, CT 06851
(617) 497-5146   (203) 846-3777

Library of Congress Catalog Card Number: 89-10669
ISBN: 0-915299-55-0

Book and jacket design by Joyce C. Weston
Typeset by Rudra Press, Cambridge, Massachusetts
Printed and bound by Arcata/Halliday
Printed in the United States of America

Library of Congress Cataloging-in-Publication Data

Tateishi, Kazuma, 1900-
    Eiennare bencha seishin. English
    The eternal venture spirit: an executive's practical philosophy/by Kazuma Tateishi

    Translation of: *Eiennare bencha seishin*
    ISBN 0-915299-55-0
    1. Industrial management — Japan.   2. Industrial management.   I. Title.
HD70.J3T3813   1989   89-10669
658.4'001 — dc20
CIP

89   90   91   10   9   8   7   6   5   4   3   2   1

Contents

Publisher's Foreword

THE OLD way of doing business just isn't working for us anymore. No longer is the American market protected from international competition. "Made in America" is not what it used to be. Today, we are in need of a new paradigm to carry us successfully into the future.

Our whole thought process about how to operate in business has to change. What is taught in our business schools has to change. The way management functions through authoritative structures, ignoring customer needs and desires and employees aspirations and perceptions, also must change if we are to be successful in this highly competitive world. The fundamental techniques of how we motivate and inspire people to their personal greatness must change, now and in the future.

In the past, there was no real competition for American industry — we simply dominated the field. Today, we confront a whole new competitive atmosphere, one that requires a vastly different kind of educated worker. Training has been left to the formal education system. Corporations now, however, must take more responsibility for educating all of their members.

A whole new lexicon of management terminology has emerged with words like corporate culture, participative management, ownership, teamwork, entrepreneurship. People want and expect to find such ideas implemented in their work environment today.

We need new leaders with a new consciousness to make such a shift; we need a whole new spirit of the enterprise, a new spirit of membership.

Vision, purpose, structure, strategy, and daily activities are so interrelated that they must function together or growth cannot occur for an organization, nor for individuals.

It is easy to make the mistake of equating expansion in numbers with growth. But if numbers grow without integrating the purpose, the daily task, and the long-term strategies that link them, then success can only occur in short-term bursts. Investments in people will be lost. Investments in technology will be inadequate over time and therefore wasted. Profits must benefit a much wider range of people with vested interests in the organization's success: the stockholders, the employees, the community, the customers, the vendors — everyone.

People are the generative power of an organization, its primary source of creative ideas. Total quality and customer service, effective structures to support long-term needs, integration of functions, and decentralization of management are the survival kit for future business.

Yet implementing these structures in an organization for some reason seems to become almost impossible. Pressures of short-term crises, fluctuations in financial conditions, fear of relinquishing control, inability to accept failure as a necessary part of lasting improvement — all these become obstacles for establishing a system whose daily activities relate to a company's direction and long-term success.

In *The Eternal Venture Spirit*, Kazuma Tateisi demonstrates the wisdom of a long-term perspective. He tells us the story of building a multibillion dollar company from underneath the rubble of the war and the pain of personal loss and business decline. As the story unfolds, we realize that his success is founded on a totally new business paradigm.

Tateisi's paradigm consists of three commitments: to serve the needs of the customer and society; to continually develop leading-edge technology; and to increasingly decentralize management structures.

During the three decades in which this story unfolds, Tateisi focused on serving the customer with quick response and innovative products. He established business relationships that addressed critical social needs. He created structures that forced competent decision-making and effective delegation of authority.

As a result of Kazuma Tateisi's wisdom and long-range understanding, Omron Tateisi Electronics has achieved astounding growth and lasting success in its highly competitive field. We encourage all senior managers to read this simple little book with the amazement and respect with which we have produced it. It provides a model for much more than financial success; it provides a paradigm for business to become an integrative force in our rapidly changing world.

We wish to offer our gratitude to Mr. Kazuma Tateishi and to Mr. Katsuyoshi Saito of Diamond Publishing for using Productivity Press as their English publisher. Special thanks also go to our skillful production team, David Lennon and Esmé McTighe, for the care they took to make this a beautiful book; to Joyce C. Weston for the cover design; and to our friends at Rudra Press for their consistently excellent typesetting and layout efforts.

Norman Bodek
President

Diane Asay
Editor

Preface to the American Edition

I first met Kazuma Tateisi exactly thirty years ago, at the very beginning of my first Japanese lecture and consulting trip in June 1959. The trip started with a three-day top-management seminar in the Hakone mountains. Sitting at the back of the room among the fifty participants, all top executives of major companies, was a very thin man who said nothing even during the rather animated small-group sessions. Only when the rest of the group seemed to be either totally bored or openly skeptical would he suddenly spring to life. When I remarked that a business had to have a mission, a vision, and a clear sense of what it contributed to society and economy, most participants appeared bored with what to them were clearly mere platitudes. But the quiet man at the back of the room nodded vigorously and began to take notes furiously.

A little later I tried to illustrate a point by making a comparison between the treatment of space in Japanese painting and in Western painting. The executives looked baffled; clearly they knew neither Japanese nor Western art. But the quiet man in the back of the room laughed out loud and again began to take notes furiously. When I stressed that to be a major economic power Japan would have to develop its own modern technology rather than depend on joint ventures and technology imports, my listeners protested, politely but sharply. "Japan," they argued, "was far too poor, far too backward, far too young as a modern economy to do anything but depend on the technology of the advanced West." The lone dissenter was the quiet man in the back of the room; indeed he suddenly spoke up — to everyone's surprise — and said, "You are absolutely right; and it's high time we did it." Who was this interesting fellow? I was told that "he is a small manufacturer from Kyoto, quite unimportant; he makes industrial controls. He'll never get anywhere; he refuses to join any of the big industrial groups." Clearly, this was an unusual man. I accepted gladly when he invited me to visit him in Kyoto.

A few weeks later I spent a Sunday with the Tateisi family in their Kyoto home. It was a visit I have never forgotten, for its warmth, for its happiness, and for all I learned. All the Tateisi children were there; they ranged from grown people, already married, to a small boy still in elementary school. As I told my wife in a letter written after I returned to my hotel, they were the warmest and happiest family I have ever met. Kazuma Tateisi, the father, was a wonderful host. He introduced me to the Noh play — he is an accomplished chanter — making me an instant addict of this great and powerful art. Since he knew of my interest in Japanese painting, he showed me some of his own highly accomplished watercolors and drawings, which wittily combine Japanese tradition and modern Western aesthetics. Above all, he talked of his company and of his plans for it. The company was then quite small, having barely recovered from wartime destruction. Tateisi himself was no longer a young man; indeed, at fifty-nine he was well past the traditional Japanese retirement age. Nevertheless, he foresaw a company that was at the leading edge of advanced technology and was operating world-wide. Above all, he had a clear sense of the company's mission. It was to use the tools of cybernetics and automation — both dreams rather than technologies in those days — to change the economy from one of toil to one fueled by knowledge, thus freeing the worker to concentrate on tasks of mind and spirit. Of course, John Diebold and Norbert

Weiner had already written on similar topics, but here was an industrialist and businessman actually _acting_ on this vision, as I saw the following day when he took me through his small plant.

I had already realized that Japan would stage a remarkable economic comeback (my first article on the subject was written only a few weeks later, after my return home to the United States). I became convinced of this, however, after visiting the Tateisi home and plant. "If this man lives," I wrote to my wife, "Japan will become a major economic power in no time. The only trouble is, he is already almost sixty and seems to be quite frail."

Well, he did live. Moreover, he built the company he so clearly envisaged all of thirty years ago. In this book he has spelled out his achievement and the philosophy underlying it. He does not dwell on his own remarkable story — growing up in deepest poverty; working his way through an unpretentious technical college far from Tokyo; refusing to do the "obvious" and take a job with an established big company but starting out on his own as a penniless inventor; barely surviving World War II and its destruction; beginning all over again; spurning all offers to go into joint ventures or to import technology; and, eventually creating a two and a half billion-dollar company, a true multinational that is at the cutting edge of automation and control technologies. Rather, Kazuma Tateisi presents in this book the basic creed that underlay his success. While the story itself is a Japanese story — there were other, similarly successful Japanese entrepreneurs and business builders, such as Honda, or Matsushita of Panasonic and National — the Tateisi entrepreneurial philosophy and business principles have universal application and should have universal appeal.

Peter F. Drucker
Author and Management Consultant
Claremont, California

Preface to the Japanese Edition, 1985

KAZUMA Tateisi's *The Eternal Venture Spirit* is not merely a tour de force in its own right; it is also a treasure house of valuable learning for administrators. More than any related work I have seen to date, Mr. Tateisi's book makes clear the difference between "administration" and "management." The former is defined as a kind of "feed-forward" operation that foresees company prospects and establishes company direction. This is a penetrating observation, one that I would wish could be read by all administrators who have come to feel that their job is merely to oversee others and keep track of the overall organization.

When Mr. Tateisi speaks of his own administrative experience, the reader cannot help but be aware of his age. His wife passed away in 1950, leaving him and his seven children at great loss. That same year, the company was only a step away from bankruptcy and reduced its employees to just thirty-three. Mr. Tateisi is 89 this year, so we can see that these incidents took place when he was in his fiftieth year.

I wonder how many middle-aged executives today would, under similar circumstances, resolve to build a multi-billion-dollar company, become so passionately enthusiastic about new words as Tateisi was about *automation* and *cybernetics*, and seek new challenges at every turn? How many would buy such a new gadget as a Sony transistor radio and find in it inspiration for a new product, as Tateisi found his inspiration for a contactless switch? How most of us, in the face of diversity, lose the desire to take up a new challenge!

During the decade previous to publication of the first edition of this work, I had the opportunity to discuss a wide range of business topics with Mr. Tateisi. His insight, comprehension, and retentiveness surpass that of most administrators in their prime. Such mental youthfulness cannot be attributed merely to Western medicine. Tateisi apparently derives his motivational force from his relish in taking risks, in playing the role of challenger, and in setting "impossible" goals.

A few points about Tateisi's administrative skills deserve special mention:

1. *Like a natural scientist, Tateisi is continually observing things.*

This includes not only flow of people, money, and information, but societal phenomena as well. He possesses an extraordinary ability to detect changing aspects of the world. He continually fires off the question, "Why?," which serves as the agent for his hatching of new ideas. This inquisitive stance has born fruit in enterprises related to traffic control, railway station work, and finance, among others.

2. *Tateisi is inspired by first-rate people.*

His sphere of acquaintance is extremely broad, extending over his pastimes and artistic activities as well as his business endeavors. He has taken particular inspiration from Yoichi Ueno on automation, Katsuzo Nishi on cybernetics, and Peter Drucker on the operational division system. Strictly speaking, these three are not specialists in those respective fields. They are people he respects, and from their words he draws inspiration for the ideas he has already determined to be important.

3. *Tateisi is ahead of his time.*

In pursuing the abstract fields of automation or cybernation, he had no models. Practically all of the early projects were sketched out on the basis of an idea and an image of the future. In fact, the various excellent businesses that exist today emerged from a background of numerous failures. The credit card vending machines that Omron developed for Canteen found no market at the time. This state of affairs compelled the later strategic shift to financial terminals.

Twenty years later, however, this need is finally arising in the United States in the form of demands for card-type theater ticket vending machines and the like. Tateisi was also ten years ahead of his time in creating divisions in Omron Tateisi for electronic transactions and for information systems.

4. Tateisi puts into practice the societal responsibilities of an enterprise.

Although he speaks little of it in this book, what Tateisi has done for the handicapped was a piece of drama in itself. His approach was based on the belief that handicapped people would be able to do the same tasks as the unimpaired if their residual functions could be integrated with machines. It is a particularly humanitarian concept and one that represents a pinnacle for a "cybernetics" man. In terms of administration, Omron Taiyo Denki lies at the opposite pole from the more well-known "economic animal" image.

The eyes of Tateisi, the administrator, are without a doubt still gazing ten years ahead of his time. Add to that trait 50 years of experience in administration and in life, and you have a man whose time-frame in administration and in innovation surely exceeds by far that of the ordinary manager. In this book he not only suggests ways to ward off the "big-business syndrome" but also outlines a philosophy that will no doubt retain its relevance for generations to come.

I am particularly pleased that *The Eternal Venture Spirit* will, by this new edition, be shared with readers of English. We in Japan are known to seek out all we can absorb of the knowledge and the ways of other peoples of the world. We translate vast storehouses of learning from other languages into Japanese. And we have much also to share with other peoples, but so much of that never leaves the Japanese language. Fortunately, English speaking people who are interested in Japan and Japanese business can now take learning from *The Eternal Venture Spirit* of Mr. Tateisi, a worthy Japanese role model.

Kenichi Ohmae
Director
McKinsey & Company, Inc.

List of Illustrations

The Eternal Venture Spirit
An Executive's Practical Philosophy

PART ONE

Big-Business Syndrome

CHAPTER ONE

Diagnosis

IN mid-1983 we at Omron Tateisi Electronics carried out a corporate reorganization to eradicate a disease that had wormed its way into Omron — a sickness I call *big-business syndrome*.

A few years earlier, Japanese newspapers and magazines had been full of discussions about this affliction of private enterprise. They called it variously the "British disease" or the "French disease."

Big-business syndrome can be recognized by the following symptoms: a highly centralized and swollen bureaucracy, a proliferation of special forms and permits to handle routine decisions, increasing numbers of meetings to reach decisions, and transference of problems between departments. Final decisions are put off because executives are unwilling to accept specific responsibility. As a result, communications and instructions to the front line, the actual site of the problem, are delayed indefinitely until oversight turns into authority. Such erosion of an organization's ability to respond destroys any mindset of efficiency that may have existed before (Figure 1).

I first noticed these symptoms at Omron in the fall of 1981. Perhaps it was a founder's intuition that told me something was amiss.

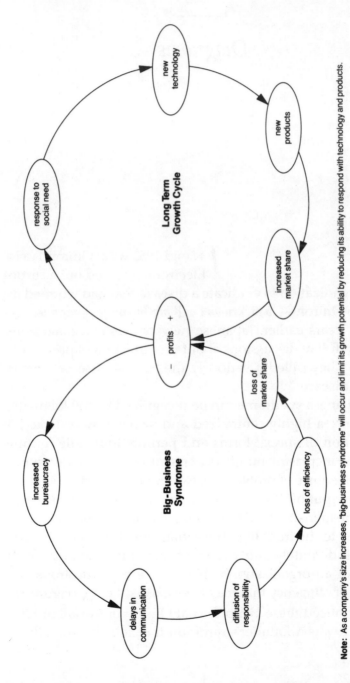

Note: As a company's size increases, "big-business syndrome" will occur and limit its growth potential by reducing its ability to respond with technology and products.

Figure 1. Big-Business Syndrome — a natural result of growth

As I paid closer attention, I noticed that internal response had slowed appreciably. When inventory was swollen, for example, even specific orders to "reduce inventory" could not cause it to subside readily. I noticed, too, that response to external demands was much slower. Our ability to respond quickly to customers' requests had eroded.

When we were smaller and a customer asked us to modify a product or create one that would meet an immediate need, the sales representative would quickly report the demand, whereupon the technicians would make the parts without any drawings. If the assembled prototype looked satisfactory, it would be taken straight to the customer; the preliminaries would be settled; and we'd have the order on the spot. The whole process would take less than two weeks. By the early 1980s, however, we had grown enough that two or three months were required for such a transaction.

Customers have all sorts of plans in the works, and their requests require timely response. If we do not meet their needs quickly, they'll go to someone who can.

In the control equipment business, the mainstay of Omron's operations, the 40 percent market share that we had relied on through the late 1970s had fallen in less than five years to 37 percent. The key reason for this decline was a steady loss of customers precipitated by slow response to their demands — an increasing lag between customer needs and new product development or improvement.

This was clearly a symptom of big-business syndrome. I shuddered to think what would happen if this slow responsiveness were to run its course. We might never recover. Once the dawdling has begun, there is the danger of a swift plunge into bankruptcy.

Dread of the Painless Disease

If we think of diseases of the human body, it is those which do not hurt that are often the most dangerous. In many forms of cancer, for instance, it is only the later stages of the disease that are extremely painful.

Similarly, big-business syndrome is a chronic illness unaccompanied by pain in its early stages. Furthermore, the pain felt on the actual operating line tends not to be transmitted to the top echelons, making it quite dangerous. For example, when a customer whose orders are worth $100,000 per year is lost because of the slow response of a senior manager, it is the salesperson on the front line who will feel the pain.

When an organization becomes too big and complex — when information flowing from the contact site to the top must pass through several steps, and when the meetings go on interminably — then the pain loses its sharpness along the way. Particularly malignant is the existence at every level of those who, in order to protect their own positions, will not pass bad news on to their superiors. When problems are concealed from the top, then the executives will not appreciate the seriousness of the customer loss. Thus the problem becomes chronic, eventually costing the company its competitiveness.

Indeed, it was clear that a fundamental reason for Omron's loss of market share was the top echelon's unawareness of pain on the front line.

The Vice of Unanimity

Major problems related to big-business syndrome also arise at the highest level of the decision-making framework.

The highest decision-making organ at Omron had been the management committee of the board of directors, consisting of the nine senior directors, who met twice a month. Various measures submitted for approval to the management committee would become bulky reports by the time they passed through the meetings of department heads and division managers.

Moreover, since there were so many steps, a great deal of time passed before proposals would be presented to the management committee. Furthermore, if some element of a proposal seemed incomplete, someone would move that it be sent back for redrafting. A decision on that item would be put off until the next meeting or the one after that, and so two weeks or a month would slip by.

This problem even reached as far as the three executive managing directors who were in charge of development, production, and marketing. The system called for the executive director to serve as an adviser, consultant, and coordinator to the line, not to exercise direct control over the worksite. In practice, however, when the director offered advice about what should be done, it was viewed from below as a direct order. The chain of command thus became confused, creativity on the line was stymied, and communication about problems broke down.

Another problem related to the role of the president, who chaired the meetings of the management committee. Theoretically, final decisions were his, but often the collective will of directors took on greater weight in the decision. Again, responsibility was not clearly delineated.

Further, the division head, called in to give a presentation to the management committee, would often bring along the department head directly in charge of the matter at hand. After making some introductory remarks, the division head would have the department head explain the proposal. Since the division chief was supposed to have given the matter enough study to be able to make the presentation himself, we were not very pleased to see him use his subordinate as a proxy.

Another problem was that line officers at the division-head level could not converse directly with chief executives. Even if they attended the directors' meeting to present a proposal, they had no chance for an actual dialogue with the chairman or the president.

In the end, tasks remained half completed and responsibility was obscured. The result was a mentality of diffused responsibility, and an inflexible and unresponsive system based on a false need for unanimity.

The bigger a company gets, the stronger is the tendency among its executives to decide things unanimously. When that tendency takes over, then decisions on matters that generate even the slightest dissension may be postponed indefinitely. The postponed decision eventually becomes an everyday occurrence. If meetings are held only once a month, then the decision is put off for an entire month.

When it comes to taking responsibility for a decision, I have always advocated use of the *70/30 rule*. For example, let's say the initiation of a new branch of operations is proposed: If there seems to be 70 percent confidence in the venture, then it's a go. The 30 percent of doubt should stimulate thinking about what kind of measures to take if things should turn out badly. This is known as a calculated risk.

One must launch a project with bold execution. A decision without risk is not really a decision at all.

In light of today's rapid transitions, the 70/30 rule may even be too limiting. There might be times when a 30/70 rule is best to follow.

I have found that failure to implement the 70/30 rule throughout the company, from the board of directors down, is an invitation to slow response.

The Union Leaders' Foreboding

"People don't usually like to talk about trouble, but since things have come this far, I think you all should be aware of what's going on." These were my words to a group of union leaders at an informal labor-management meeting in early 1983. I went on to put forward my view that big-business syndrome was eating into the company.

For the past four or five years, Omron has been losing market share in control equipment, which is our lifeblood. We've slipped from our old 40 percent level down to 37 percent. Now, what is the meaning of a three-percent drop in market share? Today's automation market is worth about ¥300 billion per year. Since our company has been one of the pioneers of automation, we have built that market with our own blood and sweat. And now we have passively handed three percent over to second- and third-ranking makers. Three percent is about ¥9 billion, and if we allow half of that for markup, then we've lost close to ¥4.5 billion in hard-earned profit.

The most significant cause of this has been slowness in new product development. Our lagging response to user needs has driven away even some of our steady customers. Those who have been feeling the pain most keenly are you salesmen on the front line. Since we can't meet the customers' demands, you have to look on passively while rival makers snatch away our valued customers. All you can do is stand there and bite your thumbs. The front line is screaming with pain. Meanwhile, the corporate structure is so swollen that it cannot feel the pain. That, you see, is the fundamental characteristic of the big-business syndrome now attacking our company.

That said, we adjourned to a small restaurant in Kyoto, where the executives and the union officials exchanged views while plucking food from a hotpot. The opinion of the young union leaders came as a surprise.

"Mr. Tateisi, we were very glad to hear what you said today."

"How can you be happy to hear such bad news?"

"Well, you see, we stopped worrying about that sort of thing long ago. After all, why should we think the higher-ups were concerned? If they had been really worried, they would have *done* something, but they never did. So even if we were apprehensive, it couldn't be helped. But today, none other than the chairman of the board himself sounded the alarm — and offered a prescription for curing the problem. Now we know that the people at the top are sincerely worried, and that's why we are happy."

When I heard that, I was happy, too. As long as we had a lot of these fervid young types around, and if we played our cards right, we could surely revitalize Omron.

A few days later the Omron Development Club, a nationwide organization of sales agents, held their New Year's reception at the Tokyo Prince Hotel. After the special guests had left, I gave the insiders the same speech that I had given to the union leaders; immediately afterward I was surrounded by seven or eight sales representatives who were just as delighted as those young union reps had been.

I put some questions to them.

"So what's up? Isn't Thanks chewing into your photoelectric-switch business?" (Thanks was a photoelectric-switch venture business in Nagoya with about 300 employees.)

"It's outrageous, sir. They aren't chewing into us, they're swallowing us whole."

I was overwhelmed. During the past few years even I had heard about how Thanks had grabbed market share by moving boldly into the gaps in the Omron product line. But that wasn't all, as I now learned. On countless orders, even when customers were looking for difficult labor-saving improvements, the venture firm had dealt with the problems, won the customers' hearts, and gobbled up more of our business.

To put it plainly, the robust vitality of this venture business called Thanks was exactly the same sort of strength that Omron had thrived on thirty years earlier.

That golden age was the 1960s, during which Omron established its reputation as a research-and-development company. It began with our development in 1960 of a contactless proximity switch, the world's first application of semiconductors to control technology, and an innovation that lent considerable impetus to the ongoing electronics revolution. It continued with our independent development in 1963 of cybernation (computerized control technology) — clearly an innovation — which we subsequently used to pioneer systems such as traffic-control networks, automated railway stations, and on-line banking machines.

The following episode is a good example of the entrepreneurial spirit that engendered that golden age.

A Prototype in Four Days

In 1955, the curtain went up on Japan's era of home appliances. A company called Tokyo Tsushin Kogyo (now known as Sony) introduced the world's first five-band super transistor radio, and in the next few years televisions, washing machines, mixers, and a wide variety of other electrical products flooded the market.

Between 1955 and 1970 Omron grew from its position as Kyoto's premier electrical-parts maker into a much larger firm. We were responsible for the inauguration of Japan's automation market. We advanced resolutely into the market of home-appliance industries, and we stimulated the demand for automation devices linked to the revolutions of technological innovation and cost consciousness in manufacturing.

The product that started us on this path was the home pump pressure switch, which is still being manufactured at our Kurayoshi plant.

At that time, Mr. Tanahashi, who is now the director of our System Engineering Research Laboratory, was a novice salesman and the sole staff member of a branch store in the Umegaecho neighborhood of Osaka. There he had the following conversation with one of our senior managing directors, Shiro Fukui, who was on his way home from a business trip.

"Sir, a little while ago, a man from a company called Sanyo Electric came in and bought a couple of micro-switches."

"Sanyo? You don't say! Tell me more."

"I explained some of the microswitch applications that are written up in the catalog, like how they can be used as washing machine door switches or pump pressure switches, and then he bowed politely and left. Are you familiar with that company, sir?"

"You mean you don't even know about a company as big as that? You'd better march straight over there with some of our products!"

His ears still smarting from the unexpected tongue-lashing, Tanahashi rushed out to Sanyo the next morning and gave them a detailed explanation of the switches, whereupon they asked him to come back a few days later. When he returned, they spread in front of him a blueprint for a home-use automatic pump and asked, "Can you give us a pressure switch in four days?"

Tanahashi's first thought was "That's absurd!" but after a moment's reflection he answered, "We'll do our best." At that time, I had been thoroughly inculcating the employees with such imperatives as "Meet the deadline!" and "The customer has top priority!" It was becoming standard procedure to work through the night if necessary to meet the supply deadline, even if the order was a little unreasonable.

When Tanahashi brought in the drawings and explained the situation to me, I gave the order to get it done immediately. It was at this point that I resolved firmly to move into the home appliance industry. I called in the managers and gave them the following message:

"This pressure switch has convinced me that we should go after the home appliance industry in a big way. It's an industry that's famous for cost-cutting, so with our present cost capabilities we might have to shed some blood at first. But we shouldn't be afraid of that. On the contrary, this is our chance to elevate our capabilities in cost efficiency, production methods, and sales techniques."

The research and development corps was still rather small, but the workers went all-out to develop that pressure switch. They devised a four-sided rubber bellows, a cast-zinc case, and so on. It was the epitome of hard work, and they had that pressure switch completed in four days!

When Tanahashi walked proudly into Sanyo and showed them the prototype, the supervisor's eyes nearly popped out of his head.

"Even though I gave you only four days, I thought it would take you ten," he said. "But somehow you got it done within the deadline."

In a single stroke, Sanyo's confidence in Omron soared. This sort of vitality powered Omron's surge forward between 1955 and the late 1960s. By 1983, however, as I realized in that conversation with the salesmen, that motive force was slipping out of the company because of big-business syndrome.

I understood then that in order to cure big-business syndrome, it was necessary for Omron to operate once again as if it were a small business.

CHAPTER TWO

Treatment

*D*ESPITE the advantages of the company's small-business days, in reality it was simply impossible for Omron, which had worked so hard to build itself up, to go back to being the smallish, 110-man enterprise that it had been in 1955. Instead, I devised a scheme that would have essentially the same effect.

I wanted Omron to operate as if each of its divisions were small businesses in themselves. I was certain that by creating several appropriately sized small divisions and carrying out a complete transfer of authority to them, I could wipe out big-business syndrome with a single stroke. Omron could return to the responsive structure I had devised in 1955 to support an initiation of the automation industry in Japan. It was a way to return to the starting point, to infuse Omron with the spirit of the entrepreneur.

I am talking about a revolution in consciousness — a revival of the venture spirit that marked Omron's high-growth years. Such a revival would enable us to conduct business in a freewheeling manner without heavy pressure from above and to make unlimited use of natural talents. We would return to the style of work in which one is constantly absorbed in ingenious schemes. My hope was for a revival of that golden era of research and development, when Omron was ablaze with energy throughout, and major new products were created one after another.

We implemented a corporate restructuring plan in June 1983. At the time we had about 5,300 employees.

To infuse in everyone's consciousness the spirit behind this restructuring, we chose three slogans for everyone to repeat daily: "everyone sells," "quick response," and "quick action." Each morning, when employees met each other for the first time of the day, they were to recite these slogans instead of the normal greetings, so that the ideas would be fixed in their minds as they went about their business.

There were two pillars of the restructuring plan. One was to bring top management closer to actual working conditions. The other was to create several appropriately sized divisions that would be given complete autonomy and would operate as small businesses within the company.

Blitz Tactics at the Top

First, to bring the top executives closer to actual working conditions, we abolished the top decision-making body, the nine-member management committee of the board of directors. In its place we created an executive committee consisting of the three top officers of the company — the chairman, the president, and the vice-president. While the management committee had been meeting twice monthly, the streamlined executive committee, adopting as its motto "lightning attack," began meeting once each week.

The three executive committee members are the representative directors who, through their individual decisions and actions, bear legal responsibility for the company's internal and external dealings. The deliberations, modifications, and decisions of these three executives are naturally the supreme power of the company, from which all other authority flows. Moreover, their decisions are made very quickly. When a proposal is sent to the committee from the division level, it will definitely be decided upon within one week. Implementation of "quick response" begins with the top executives!

Furthermore, if there seems to be a problem with a division or its staff, the committee does not have to wait for measures to be drafted and presented from below. They can call in the chief of the division or of the headquarters that oversees a set of divisions, and receive reports and advice directly. A decision can then be made on the spot. Sometimes a division sends a request via the president's office for a dialogue with the executive committee. Depending on the nature of the problem, these consultations may last as long as a couple of hours or even half a day. Even rather troublesome matters can usually be disposed of within a half day.

When the executive committee makes a decision, it does not give orders for its implementation. Such responsibility and authority are completely delegated to the divisions. Rather, the executive committee acts like a consulting, advisory body.

With this arrangement, I was able to make excellent use of the executive know-how that I had built up over nearly 50 years of experience. This was not limited to advising the division heads; through the executive committee it became possible for me to transmit my accumulated wisdom regarding executive decision-making to the presidential and vice-presidential level. This had not been possible under the previous management committee setup.

Previously, I had always attended the management committee meetings, but merely as one of the members. Actually, as chairman my role was more that of a "prompter," as in Japanese Noh drama. In a Noh play, when the leading actor forgets some of the words of his chant, there is a prompter on stage who instantly supplies the necessary words. The actor seldom forgets, but the prompter has to be ready to step in at any moment. Thus, the prompter has to know the material as well or better than the actor. At management committee meetings, then, I served for three or four years as "prompter" to the president.

Actually, if a deficiency were to arise during a management committee meeting, it wasn't feasible to prompt in such a direct manner. As chairman I had to keep a slightly lower profile than the CEO. It wasn't appropriate for me to blurt out my opinions. If the president and I differed on some point, we couldn't very well argue our positions in front of the committee without endangering each other's credibility. In that setting the president, who chairs the meeting, and I, the chairman of the board and a mere prompter at the meeting, stand on different stages politically.

In the new structure, however, the three members of the executive committee — the chairman, president, and vice-president — all stand on the same stage, thus making possible frank exchanges. My 50 years of experience could be put to full use, and the president could acquire on-the-job training. The executive committee system, by the way, is quite effective for executive training.

Venture Management by Decentralization

The small-division system, which is the other pillar of the reorganization plan, was designed to consist of divisional headquarters based on our primary markets. These head divisions served as umbrellas over the various product divisions. The intent was to stimulate venture management by creating a series of small and medium-sized companies within the large company.

Most of our key competitors were small companies of strong vitality — so-called venture businesses. By thoroughly decentralizing authority into small-business divisions, we made each of our operations about the same scale as that of its rivals. If the main competitor had something like two or three hundred employees, then our corresponding unit would have at most four or five hundred persons. Our aim was to make the opposing forces of more or less equal size and to foster a change in consciousness by whipping up a mentality of rivalry.

On the basis of that thinking, we first created a divisional headquarters for each of our four main markets: control components, electronic fund transfer systems, public service systems, and office automation systems.

Within the Control Components Division, which provides about 70 percent of our total sales, eleven small divisions were set up. In each of the other fields, two divisions were set up. Three additional, independent divisions were established: the Health and Medical Equipment Division; the Industrial Control Systems Division; and the Semiconductor Manufacturing Equipment Division (abolished in 1984). In sum, we created twenty divisions — twenty venture businesses within the company (Figures 2 and 3).

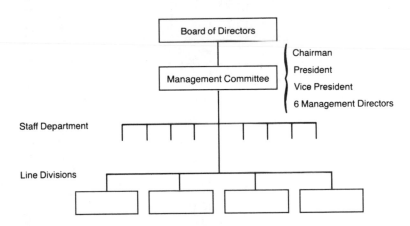

Figure 2. Old Organization Structure

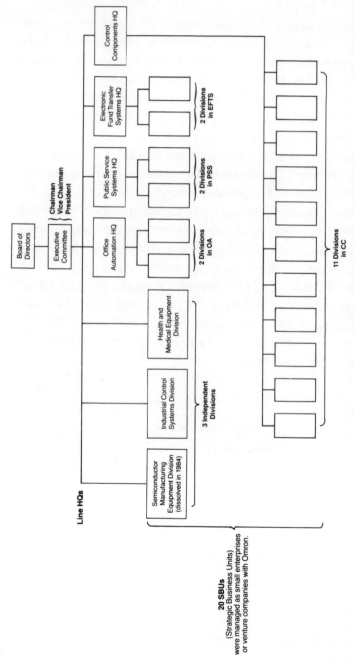

Note: Management Committee was abolished and Executive Committee consisting of the three top officers was organized; the decentralized management system was introduced and higher responsibility was transferred to each SBU manager.

Figure 3. Decentralized Organization Chart of 1983

These 20 "medium-sized businesses," or strategic business units (SBU), were commissioned to perform everything from research and development to production, domestic marketing, and even overseas marketing. Previously the business divisions had not been responsible for research and development. This function had been split between the Central Research Laboratory, responsible for long-range work, and the Development Technology Centers, in charge of medium- and short-range projects. One of the goals of the restructuring was to give the divisions as much as they could handle of the short-range product development. We believed that when it came to things such as the improvement of existing products, the divisions that handled manufacturing had a much greater store of expertise.

Until that time, overseas marketing had been carried out by an overseas marketing division, but in the restructuring, employees of that division were reassigned among the various strengthened divisions. Under the old system, when an order was issued from one of our sales subsidiaries in North America, Europe, or Southeast Asia, it went first to the Overseas Marketing Division, then to the division that produced the product, and finally to the actual factory. That lengthy route was replaced by a "hotline" system of direct communication between the overseas companies and the factories (Figure 4).

Overseas marketing division personnel who were proficient in foreign languages were reassigned to the factories. Now, whether the incoming request is for an estimate, a confirmation of delivery time, or new product information, the response is so much faster that the old system does not even bear comparison.

Our employees used to think of exporting as a sideline. They had their hands full taking care of sales in Japan, and they thought of exports as simply an additional windfall. In such an atmosphere a slow response to an overseas order was natural.

Today, however, there is no need to make such a distinction between domestic business and exporting. Communications

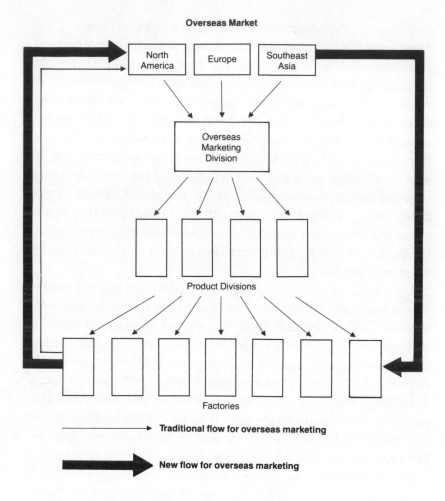

Figure 4. Overseas Marketing

technology has made wonderful progress. If we use this technology for direct "hotline" relationships between overseas subsidiaries and factories, then doing business in New York, Paris, or Milan is no different from our domestic business. Of course, nothing can be done about the physical distance involved — large stocks of products are required overseas for timely order fulfillment. But aside from the international shipping procedures, exporting is no different from domestic shipping. At any rate, since Omron has about 40 percent of the domestic market in control components, isn't it reasonable to expect that, with the proper marketing capabilities, we might achieve a 30 percent share of that market overseas?

The Theory of Provided Conditions

Along with the widening of the divisions' scope of activities came a significant expansion of the division managers' responsibility and authority.

Every aspect of my remedy for big-business disease was based on the "theory of provided conditions." Briefly, this theory states simply that "if you want to create a certain result, you must first create the conditions that will absolutely force that result to occur."

Traditional structures are based on a "meritocratic" school of thinking. This approach holds that first, an elite corps must be trained, and from that group a few are picked who will be expected to provide the desired results. That procedure alone is not enough, however. The fact that an enterprise must *train* an elite corps indicates that the structure is insufficient to produce the necessary qualities of maturity in its people. An optimum structure will promote the emergence of qualified leaders.

Thus, I reversed the usual procedure. First, a small number were picked to lead the divisions; the structure then forced them to take leadership responsibility whether they liked it or not.

Previously, the division manager was expected to take responsibility only for profit and loss. He could do his job by simply keeping his eye on the sales total and the profit margin. With the restructuring, however, he was made responsible for the balance sheet and cash flow as well. In short, the division manager was assigned a task similar to that of the president of a medium-sized company.

The corporate financial headquarters — operating like the "Omron Bank" — maintains accounts that are regarded as loans to the various divisions. If the inventory in a certain division has increased compared to its level a year earlier, then that increase will be considered to be an additional loan from the "Omron Bank"; and interest will be charged at the going rate, say, 7.2 percent.

In this respect, the division operates like an independent, medium-sized business. Moreover, since the division has responsibility for everything from research and development to production, and for both domestic and international marketing, it has been reborn as a venture business that is directly comparable to its competitors.

In the theory of provided conditions, the first step is to create the conditions under which the desired result will have to happen. The corporate restructuring was the means by which Omron carried out that initial step — creating the conditions whereby the divisions had no choice but to become venture businesses.

The First Year of the New System

When I looked back a little more than a year after implementing the new structure, I could see that clear progress had been made in revolutionizing consciousness. By filling the air with the "quick response" and "quick action" slogans that were substituted for morning greetings among employees, these ideas had gradually permeated our business habits.

Evidence of the change occurred in several ways. For one thing, the standard amounts of time required to fulfill a customer's specifications for some new item became precisely fixed. Employees identified which modifications would take several days, which designs would take a week, and which prototype developments would take three months. Also, through facsimile communication with overseas sales offices, prompt response to an overseas query became as much the rule as was prompt response to a domestic query. The traditional misguided notion that "exports are naturally slower" had been reformed.

Seeing these and many other changed conditions, I pronounced that big-business syndrome had been 70 percent cured.

The improvement was visible in the business results reported for fiscal year 1984, ending March 31 (Figure 5).

Fiscal year 1984 began under the old system. At the beginning of the term, an annual sales total of ¥187.1 billion (then approximately $800 million) was projected. This figure was arrived at by extrapolating a 14-percent increase over the previous year's sales. However, since we effected the restructuring in June 1983, in November the figure was revised to ¥200.3 billion. At that point I thought we had licked big-business syndrome; and growth accelerated even more. In January the estimate was again increased, to ¥205 billion, and at year's end the actual sales figure for fiscal year 1984 was ¥208.8 billion. That was some 27 percent higher than the previous year's performance. This was evidence of the revolution in consciousness that resulted from the restructuring.

1984 FY		
	Projection	Results
Sales	181.7 (141%)	208.8 (127%)
Income Before Tax	12.3 (106%)	15.3 (133%)
Net Income	6.0 (117%)	7.7 (149%)

Note: Unit = Billion Yen. Figure in ( ) shows the % increase from the previous year

Figure 5. 1984 Fiscal Report

CHAPTER THREE

Remnants of Big-Business Syndrome

*I*F big-business syndrome was 70 percent cured, then conversely, it was still 30 percent endemic. One aspect of the remaining symptoms was apparent in the financial projections for fiscal year 1985.

Sales for fiscal year 1985 were expected to grow about 20 percent from the fiscal year 1984 level. That was significantly lower, however, than the 27 percent increase that had been reflected in the 1984 figure. If we had managed 27 percent sales growth that year as a result of the restructuring, then why was such a pullback projected for the next year?

I immediately said to the division managers, "This seems strange. Why is the rate of growth so much lower?"

"Last year we overdid it," they replied. "We grew a little too much. Twenty percent will be enough for this year."

I pressed on with my questions. "So compared with last year, do you think business conditions will be better or worse?"

"Conditions will probably be better this year."

"If conditions are better than last year, why should the growth rate go down? Don't be foolish. I think we'd better rethink that projection."

27

I directed that a new plan be drawn up.

From my vantage point there was no reason to expect less than a 30 percent rate of sales growth for fiscal year 1985. Indeed, during the first few months of calendar year 1984, sales figures consistently ran about 40 percent higher than corresponding figures for the previous year.

That the aggregate projection from the various divisions should be as low as 20 percent seemed to indicate an overly cautious mindset that grows out of self-defense mechanisms. Estimates rise up through three levels of an organization, from the actual business sites to the division managers, and at each step 3 percent of the growth projection somehow evaporates. By the time fiscal year projections reach the top they have been lowered in total by 9 percent. Therefore, the sales growth projection should have been about 30 percent.

When this sort of thing occurs, it must be concluded that the attitudes of big-business syndrome are still present.

The High Growth Beneath Low Growth

In his book *Megatrends*, which was released in Japanese in April 1983, John Naisbitt pointed out that companies were right in the middle of a trend of "qualitative change from the manufacturing company to the information company." A company riding that megatrend would have the potential for high growth in the future.

Omron was definitely astride that megatrend, facing a new era of high growth comparable to the high-growth decade of the late 1960s and early 1970s. That was my basic perception in 1984. The general perception within the company was exactly the opposite, however. To remove the remnants of big-business syndrome, I first had to confront a perceptual problem about growth rate expectations and Omron's situation.

As a result of the oil crises of the 1970s and the subsequent period of lower growth, everyone in Japan had fallen into a slow-growth mentality. There was a widespread delusion that since the gross national product had expanded at a rate of 3 to 5 percent annually, then single-digit annual growth should be the rule for corporations in general, and a 10-percent rate of growth would be splendid. The tendency at Omron to think that 20-percent growth was "enough," giving no special notice to the illogic of its being lower than the previous year's rate, was a manifestation of big-business syndrome.

The 5-percent growth of the gross national product should not be used as a yardstick for individual companies. While some companies in structurally depressed industries will undoubtedly experience negative growth, companies that are riding the megatrend may achieve growth rates of 20 to 30 percent. For our company, which was visibly riding the megatrend and clearly had created the conditions that make high growth possible, it was simply inappropriate to forecast a growth rate significantly lower than that of the previous year.

The annual projection that finally emerged was close to 30 percent. Yet because the "informationizing" of companies would be accompanied by an industrial revolution of an extremely large scale, I sincerely believed that 30 percent was still a conservative growth estimate (Figure 6).

1985 FY		
	Projection	Results
Sales	251.3 (121%)	270.5 (130%)
Income Before Tax	18.5 (121%)	17.5 (114%)
Net Income	8.8 (115%)	9.1 (119%)

Note: Unit = Billion Yen. Figure in ( ) shows the % increase from the previous year

Figure 6. 1985 Fiscal Report

Why Don't Inventories Go Down?

I also noticed a remnant of big-business syndrome in factory inventories.

Each Omron division has one or more factories, and within the company they are categorized as P factories and Neo-P factories. The initial stands for the Producer System, which was devised in 1955 and resembles the focus factory system used in the United States.

At that time, control components for automation were being developed in rapid succession. As the number of products being manufactured increased, however, we soon were producing small quantities of many different items, and production management became troublesome. To make new products profitable, Omron devoted all of its investment to the creation of a series of factories at subsidiary companies with workforces of approximately fifty people each. Each of those plants was set up for assembly-line production of large quantities of a limited number of items. Since they were separate companies, naturally they were completely self-supporting systems. This was my Producer System, and the subsidiaries' factories came to be called P factories.

Along with the proliferation of product types came a gradual increase in the number of P factories. In the spring of 1965, when Omron shares were listed on the Tokyo Stock Exchange, the exchange requested us to consolidate those subsidiaries. Thus all eight of the P factories were merged into Omron. They are known within the company to this day as P factories, but in fact they are part and parcel of the parent company.

Meanwhile, there are now some twenty-three Neo-P factories. These are factories operated by subsidiary companies and designed along the lines of the original P factories (before incorporation in 1965). Most of the Neo-P factories are situated in small cities (with populations between 30,000 and 50,000) and are joint ventures with 10 to 40 percent of the capital coming from local sources. This is known as the Neo-Producer System, in order to differentiate these factories from the older and somewhat different Producer System.

During the last few years of the 1970s I noticed a sharp contrast in terms of inventory between the P and Neo-P factories. The general pattern was that the P factories had about twice as much inventory as the Neo-P factories, which were able to keep inventory down to about one month's supply.

I looked into this situation and sent a message, loud and clear, to the division chiefs: "Reduce the P-factory inventories." Nevertheless, they didn't go down one bit. After the corporate restructuring of mid-1983, and because the consciousness revolution had made good progress among employees, I expected similar progress on inventory reduction, but just as before, the P factories had twice as much inventory as the Neo-P factories.

Why didn't those inventories go down? While the presidents of the Neo-P factories took great care when it came to costs, the P factories had discovered a gimmick. Their vouchers for parts and materials purchases were passed on to the head office and posted in the aggregate totals on the head computer, and then the finance department of the Omron head office took care of all the payments. Thus, the managers of the P factories were in the sweet situation of not having to face any issues related to costs. Consequently, they were never sincerely motivated to lighten financial burdens by reducing inventory, and they were apathetic about any increase in the amount of funds tied up in inventory. This was clearly big-business disease at work.

Financial Worries Build People

Each Neo-P factory is just like an independent business in that when cash is required, the president has to go to the bank personally and take out a loan. Nobody enjoys asking for a loan, especially these executives, who have been trained as technicians and are generally not adept at financial negotiations. Therefore, they are careful about spending money.

For the Neo-P company president, the purchase of even a single mechanical part is cause for deliberation. After all, every expenditure is a bite out of the executive's own wallet. If carelessness leads to excessive purchases of parts and supplies, then the president will be personally responsible for the resulting cash problems. This is why the Neo-P factories have low inventory levels. In some Neo-P factories the inventory level is as low as about half a month's supply.

Of course, cash worries are not limited to inventory. When business is down and orders decline, there is the specter of red ink. The prospect of going to the bank with bowed head is all the more bitter. Moreover, it will naturally lead to an increase in the break-even point.

I went around to Neo-P factories in various districts and talked with the presidents about their problems, and indeed, their worst anxieties had to do with borrowing money. When it came to raising funds, the attitude of the presidents who had come from technical backgrounds was, without exception, to bemoan the misfortune that had forced them to approach the bankers with lowered head. I know exactly how they feel, for I myself am an engineer by training who has all too much experience with financial worries.

I believe, however, that financial worries are never a useless thing. Without fail, the experience of financial worry builds character. What I have found is that the Neo-P factory presidents are of a different make than the P factory managers. It is the difference between one who has experienced financial worry and one who hasn't.

Under the new corporate structure, the division managers have essentially the same type of responsibility and authority as the presidents of medium-sized companies. In contrast to the old system, in which the division manager was account-able only for the profit-and-loss situation, the new system makes them accountable for the balance sheet and cash flow as well. Naturally, the P-factory managers are among those who now have to worry directly about finances. Although direct accountability had been one of the aims of the reorganization, the situation had remained that they were still depending on the financial headquarters to handle the money.

Consequently, in order to deal with the inventory problem, I settled on a clear method for changing the consciousness of the P-factory managers. The head office stopped dealing with cash troubles; instead, the P-factory managers themselves had to go to the banks to negotiate loans for their operation costs. The implementation of this policy was the second step in the corporate restructuring.

Through the primary tactics described in this chapter, Omron was successful in its implementation of a corporate reorganization, achieving a 70 percent cure of big-business syndrome. That still left a 30 percent level of infection. To effect a complete cure is our secondary objective from now on, and as I look toward the future I sense that we have devised the right response.

Once we have achieved that secondary goal, we will again be the Omron of old, a healthy company brimming with the venture spirit. For I truly believe that it is possible to operate a large-scale venture business.

PART TWO

A Model for Instilling the Venture Spirit

CHAPTER FOUR

A Company Without Ideals Is Like a Mariner Without Charts

*T*HE most important aspect of running a business is to make the corporate ideals clear. This provides the backbone of the business. After all, for what reason do we all go to work and apply ourselves to our jobs every day? It is vital to insure that each member of the company, from the president down to the newest employee, has the same answer for that question. A comparison of companies in which some know and some do not know the answer to the question, "What are we working for?" will reveal major differences, not only in human character but also in business results.

A story from feudal times provides a good example. Three stonemasons working at the construction site for a castle were asked, "What is your reason for working here?" and the first one answered: "I'm working so that I will have food to eat." The second one replied: "I'm working to make the stones for that stone wall." The third mason, jumped to his feet and puffing out his chest, gave this reply: "I'm working in order to finish that great castle that's going up over there."

If we were to query today's business workers, we might very well get the same three types of answers. The first answer might be phrased in these forms: "I'm working in order to eat"; "I'm working to support my wife and kids"; "I'm working so I can build a house"; or "I'm working so that I can enjoy some free time." The second might be, "I'm working to make this particular product." The third answer, given proudly, might be, "I'm working to build a better world."

The differences between those three answers are differences in attitudes toward life. Where there is a choice, one should strive to promote the consciousness of the third reply. Such consciousness imparts to employees a joy of working, a joy of development, a joy of creating, and most important, a joy of living. When this sphere has been reached, labor is elevated to the domain of art, and there is a big jump in corporate earnings.

The way that we at Omron have expressed this consciousness of "working for the benefit of human society" is through our corporate policy, which is founded on the concept of "the enterprise as public servant."

The Enterprise as Public Servant

I began to think seriously about the importance of company credos in 1955. Two years earlier, through the offices of the Japan Electrical Industry Association, I had been one of five executives of small and medium-sized electrical manufacturers chosen to visit similar companies in America. At the time we were given advice from all quarters on which companies to visit, but since everybody suggested the giant concerns like General Electric and Westinghouse, it was of no use. We were left only with the resolve to find out what the smaller electrical manufacturing firms were really like.

The key lesson I learned on that inspection trip was that the wellsprings of sturdiness in American enterprise are the frontier spirit and Christianity.

Of course, the national mood in Japan is rather different, and one could not expect to instantly infuse Japanese society with either the frontier spirit or Christianity. That being the case, I started groping for another concept that would become the backbone of our company. Then in the spring of 1956 I attended a general meeting of the Economic Benevolent Society, which had been formed by the Japanese Industry Club. There I heard the society's general secretary, Mr. Kishi, say the following words: "Executives should be aware of and fulfill social responsibilities." It struck me that I had found what I was searching for. Since an enterprise exists to provide a service to society, a policy of "the enterprise as public servant" would make an ideal conceptual backbone.

It was necessary to introduce this unfamiliar concept into the company slowly, and as chances came up I spoke about it to the various directors and managers. Finally, three years later, in 1959, I put the credo of "the enterprise as public servant" into the form of the following corporate motto:

> At work for
> a better life,
> a better world for all.

This motto was formally announced on May 10, 1959, the 26th anniversary of the founding of the company. Since then it has been the corporate ideal and the conceptual backbone of Omron. Its formation began with that trip to America in 1953 and took some five years.

After this motto was established, every aspect of management became easier. This was because it came to serve as a source of strength in expanding the company's activities.

The Spirit of the Corporate Motto

To explain the essence of this corporate motto, let me say, first, that it is the primary aim of a company to grow. It is our firm conviction that all efforts should be devoted to expanding the company, and the growth of the company is understood to mean the strengthening of its ability to make contributions to society.

In concrete terms, a growing company will be able to provide more and more employment to people of the surrounding area, and as a result, it will become a good neighbor. At the same time, the customers will be served by a good supplier, and the supplier will benefit from good customers. The customers will be further served as the company's investments in research and in capital equipment lead to the provision of better products at lower prices. Moreover, because the company will naturally act to secure a reasonable profit, some half of that profit will serve the nation in the form of taxes. The remainder will serve the employees, in the form of high wages, and the shareholders, in the form of high dividends. Finally, since the company is benefiting from the general good will of the local society, it will use a portion of its profits to return the favor by carrying out specific social services and welfare programs for the community.

Yet even before these services are considered, the company is providing contributions to society through the functions and uses of the products it sells, and these boil down to a service. This service continues as the company develops new products that offer state-of-the-art service to society. This is the thinking embodied in the Omron company motto.

As the various types of services accumulate, a better society is produced, and as a result we can all enjoy, freely and peacefully, the lives that we hope for.

The idea of service to society is most concisely summed up by the idea that those who serve society best will win the most profit. These words have a strong utilitarian flavor, however, I prefer to emphasize society's gain rather than that of the company. If a company does not provide the finest service, then there is no reason to let it continue to exist; it would be just as well to destroy that sort of company. On the other hand, the company that provides the best service to society deserves the "upkeep" required to foster its growth and we should allocate to it the highest profit. Doing so serves none other than society it-self. Put in these terms, the concept loses its harsh utilitarianism.

What is Profit for a Company

After the corporate motto defining enterprise as public ser-vice was clearly set out in 1959, the performance of Omron em-ployees visibly improved, as did the business results. It was as if the surrounding society, sensing that "this company is going out of its way to serve us," supported us, providing us with profit and allowing us to grow (Figure 7).

The relation between enterprise, profit, and service is simi-lar to the pattern found in nature among the honeybee, honey, and pollination. The honeybee flits from flower to flower, in-stinctively pursuing nectar to make honey. The flowers supply nectar to the honeybees in order to accomplish pollination. Similarly, the enterprise goes to society in its pursuit of profits. Society supplies the profits to the enterprise, and in the proc-ess secures service for itself.

	Number of Employees	Annual Sales	Profit Before Tax
1955	190	245	43
1956	366	497	84
1957	431	668	159
1958	490	802	252
1959	803	1,451	311
1960	1,369	2,314	471
1961	1,670	3,217	525
1962	1,882	3,130	429
1963	2,161	4,911	784
1964	2,514	6,188	708
1965	2,578	6,369	740

Note: Unit = Million Yen

Figure 7. Productivity Figures from 1955 to 1965

The honeybee collects nectar not with the intent to pollinate the flowers, but to make honey. The result, however, is a service to the flower. So it is with the enterprise, which in its pursuit of profits ends up serving society. Therefore, to say that an enterprise is a public servant is not to say that its executives are interested in public service; rather, it is to say that fundamentally, enterprise *is* public service.

When I began doing business back in 1933, I was looking above all to eat, that is, to make a profit. Over the next twenty years I worked very hard to manage the company, and gradually I realized that an enterprise is a public servant. My realization of that fact is not important, however; the point is that Omron was a public servant right from the start.

To be sure, not every enterprise possesses a disposition toward public service. If a company's products are out of tune with society, then no matter how much profit it turns, and even though it provides the service of paying taxes, it is still far from being a public servant. In such a case, social responsibilities are being overlooked by executives; when they do take notice of public service, then the products will begin to be selected and developed without mistakes.

Even though an enterprise is essentially a public service, if its products are not suitable for society, then society, acting in its own defense, will regulate its environment by destroying the company. In order to avoid such a situation, it is incumbent upon the executive to maintain an awareness of social responsibility.

CHAPTER FIVE

———

Activating the
"Natural Healing Faculty"

A LONG with the credo of the enterprise as public servant, I have another basic precept for management, which is the idea of "the symptom as treatment." This is one of the main elements of the Nishi method of medicine, a method in which I have great confidence based on personal experience. The Nishi system of health consists of techniques by which the conscious mind is used to regulate the body, thereby maintaining one's physical well being. After following this method for more than 30 years, I have concluded that it is possible to apply the principles of the Nishi health method to the administration and management of business. To put it simply, the idea is that a symptom is an instinctive phenomenon manifested in order to cure an illness. In other words, it is a "natural healing faculty." This is an extremely important management philosophy, as I will explain.

The Symptom as Treatment

The Nishi method of healing was devised by Dr. Katsuzo Nishi. Modern medical science thinks of the symptom as the illness, and is thus centered on the use of specific medicines to eradicate symptoms. If a fever develops, the doctor will typically administer an antifebrile injection to bring it down. If there is pain, an anesthetic is injected. By contrast, the Nishi system of medicine thinks of the symptom as the treatment. It is based on the belief that symptoms appear in order to cure the illness, and thus seeks to make positive practical use of the symptoms.

For example, when the body temperature is high the pulse quickens. Since the amount of blood is constant, in order to cure an illness the body's internal feedback function increases the rate of blood circulation, which is normally 60 to 70 heartbeats per minute, to about 110. This is because an illness tends to be cured more quickly when the blood circulates rapidly. In other words, it is a natural healing function.

But when the fever, which has been generated specifically to speed up the blood flow, is regarded as the illness, then the temperature is artificially lowered, the pulse returns to its former rate, and the essential cause of the illness is left untreated. Since the fever quickly subsides, the child, feeling cured, resumes playing. In most cases, however, an even higher fever will result on the next day, causing much fuss.

When one catches a cold, it will subside after three days of bedrest. If a physician is consulted, it will take longer, because the physician makes the cure more difficult.

Now substitute a business for the patient. For example, when a cash flow problem develops, it is considered to be a symptom of insufficient funds. The usual response is to dash off to the bank. This is symptomatic treatment, which is likely to be ineffective in the long run. If, on the contrary, the cash flow problem is regarded as a condition that was manifested in order to cure the "illness" of insufficient funds, then one would first search out the reason for the emergence of the symptom. The range of causes is rather predictable — poor collection of accounts, an increase in the amount of claims or expenses, swollen inventory, and the like. When those factors are controlled, the illness of insufficient funds will be cured.

It's exactly the same with big-business syndrome. The natural healing function manifests various symptoms in order to cure the illness. I came to the realization that big-business syndrome is actually cause for joy.

The Usefulness of Money Problems

An enterprise might fall victim to any of various diseases, but in the case of a manufacturer the worst symptom must surely be the occurrence of inferior products. When that happens, the symptomatic response would be to reprimand and reassign the operator who made them. Such treatment can never be sufficient to eliminate shoddy goods. What is necessary is to carefully search out the root of the problem, by regarding the symptom — inferior products — as a phenomenon that was made evident in order to cure the insufficiency of the quality control system, and then apply the scalpel.

When the symptom is a financial problem, some people get flustered about a "shortage of funds," jump in their luxury cars, and rush to the bank. Such a symptomatic treatment will never cure the real illness. Because the financial symptom has come out in order to make the enterprise stronger, the only effective response is to use the symptom as the starting point for thinking about how the fundamental business structure can be repaired.

Financial symptoms are usually caused by maladies such as inferior products, poor accounts-collection, excessive materials-purchasing, too much inventory, or overuse of funds. Once such a cause is identified, it is surprisingly easy to fix.

If the cause of the financial worry is serious, say, sagging demand for products that are reaching the end of their market life, then it is necessary to spend some time devising a fundamental treatment.

With a little effort on the part of the executive, then, a financial crunch can be turned into a chance for the company to make vigorous strides forward. The question is whether or not the executive regards the symptom as treatment, and thus an occasion for joy.

The old saw speaks of "turning hardship to good fortune," but in the philosophy of Dr. Nishi, the hardship is itself viewed as good fortune, an insight I find to be profound and worthy of some consideration.

CHAPTER SIX

———

Applying the Law of
Natural Selection to Enterprise

*A*T the foundation of the Nishi medical system lies the biological law of natural selection. This is an extremely simple principle.

Every organism exists amid natural conditions. But natural conditions are not necessarily stable; they often change. The earth has existed for eons, during which time major changes have successively occurred. Because of the process of change, a species cannot continue to exist without the ability to adapt autonomically to those changes. For example, when confronted by the extreme challenges presented during the Ice Age, many types of organisms reached the limits of their adaptive capabilities and died off. Earlier, the mammoths and dinosaurs that once walked the earth met a similar fate. Unable to adapt to what must have been awful changes in the environment, they disappeared long ago.

Similarly, if a business is unable to adapt to changes in its environment — that is, to the shifting external realities of politics, economics, society, and technology — then it will succumb to those changes.

In Japan alone, countless businesses unable to adapt to changes in their environments have disappeared like bubbles. The passings go largely unnoticed. Unlike a person, a business leaves not a shred of evidence of its existence once it ceases operations.

The obverse of that sad fact is that a great many enterprises do adapt admirably to change in their environments, and thus continue to prosper. The relevance of the biological law of natural selection to business led me to use it as a law of management at Omron.

The Need for "Feed-forward"

If a company is to survive in this time of turbulent change, then its management must adapt to the changes in the business environment of politics, economics, society, and technology.

In this context, the most important task for the executive is to correctly read the changes in the external environment, thus being enabled to set the company on a track of high growth. To do that, it is necessary to predict the future. Specifically, one must devise distinct forecasts for the short-range, medium-range, and long-range future, and act to adapt the enterprise accordingly.

To predict the future, we first have to collect information. Then we analyze the information, draw conclusions, lay plans on the basis of those conclusions, and give appropriate orders to implement the plans. The person who receives those orders continually makes adjustments in his sphere of activities, a process that is comparable to feedback automation.

In feedback automation, a measurement is made to see how far off target something has veered. This information is passed back to an automatic control device, which rectifies the deficient factor. This is the process of control.

The position of the factory manager, for example, is an internal control job. If the top executive gives the order, "In your factory, let's make one billion yen worth of products this month," then the factory manager has a duty to achieve that level of production in one month. Every day, therefore, he takes a measurement to see how far away from the target he is. He obtains a report on the day's production and uses it to gauge whether or not the program is on schedule.

Generally speaking, the level of production in a factory will tend to run a little behind schedule until about the middle of the month. At that point the factory manager makes checks to determine the cause of the delay, and more often than not the cause is something like a difficulty in obtaining parts, or a shortage of labor.

The factory manager will typically go out of his way to clear up these problems just after the midpoint of the month, and then by the end of the month will achieve the scheduled production goal. In these circumstances the factory manager's control job is usually one of feedback automation.

Whereas the control job can be considered internal regulation, falling among those issues which can be handled purely within the company, the executive's management job is of a different dimension. To manage the company as a whole, the executive must deal with changes in the external environment, and thus needs a completely different order of effort. A single misstep could plunge the company into crisis.

It follows that if the management job is carried out solely on the basis of feedback, then it will always fall into a pattern of passivity. For example, if the external environment is gradually slipping into recession, the powers of a single executive will accomplish nothing. In other words, if one were to operate solely on the basis of feedback, then the company would without doubt be swallowed up by the recession. If, on the other hand, the executive sees that a recession is in the cards, then he can take appropriate steps to preserve the company.

Feedback Versus Feed-forward

During years of a high-growth economy, a business can simply carry out effective internal control, centered around feedback, and let things run their course. Sales of its products will grow steadily and the company can expand. But now that we are in a transition period with sharply fluctuating circumstances, it is no longer possible to manage a business solely with feedback-based control. A wise executive will positively and bravely anticipate the future. To do this, he must ceaselessly be looking into the future, obtaining information, analyzing it, and revising his plans. The management function, then, is one of *feed-forward automation*, which is one dimension higher than the control function.

As an example of the concept, let's consider the problem of adjusting the temperature of a room in winter. What sort of regulation mechanism is needed to maintain the room temperature at 23° C (73° F)?

In a feedback system, if the room temperature falls by a degree or two, the thermostat senses it and feeds back the difference from the programmed temperature to the automatic control device. Upon receiving the data, the control device works to increase the amount of hot air delivered into the room. As a result, the room temperature rises to slightly above 23°. When that happens, the thermostat cuts off the supply of hot air. After a while the temperature again drops below 23° and the cycle begins again.

In short, the room temperature is continually shifting but kept relatively stable at around the centerpoint of 23°. This is feedback automation. In this system, the modification occurs in response to a stimulus and thus it is a rather simple technology.

Feed-forward automation processes data in a totally different way. To begin with, it anticipates a drop in room temperature when the outdoor temperature drops. It also takes into account other factors affecting the room temperature such as the opening and closing of a door. (Experiments show that if the door is opened and closed about ten times, then the room temperature will fall by about two degrees.)

This data is linked directly with the automatic control device. Thus, if the door is opened and closed frequently, the control automatically sends in the required amount of hot air. Moreover, if the outdoor temperature goes down two degrees, it will increase the amount of hot air by the appropriate amount.

In this system, which anticipates temperature changes, the heat input is finely adjusted in advance of those changes. As a result, the range of variation in room temperature is extremely narrow. This is the sort of automatic-control system that constitutes feed-forward automation.

In managing a business, the executive must make a habit of predicting the future and adjusting the direction of the company's activities accordingly. That is, he has to operate in a feed-forward mode. Of course, feedback remains necessary on the internal-control side. What is required is a combination of feedback and feed-forward.

Action Is Easy, Theory Is Hard

As explained earlier, I base decisions on the "70/30 rule": if something seems to have a 70 percent chance of working, then I do it without hesitation. To carefully calculate the 30 percent risk, however, one must use feed-forward.

There is a saying that "action is easy, theory is hard." We tend to believe that we can't make a decision until we understand it theoretically and reach agreement on that basis. In that way, however, one may never get around to making the decision. To move on the basis of theory is in all events a difficult way to move. If you actually try something out, however, you gradually come to understand the theory. That is, moving on the basis of action is an easy way to move.

One should start, then, with the 70/30 rule for taking action. If we don't take action, we can't carry out either feedback or feed-forward.

The Theory of Social Needs

A most important part of an executive's job is to position his company in those markets that will have the strongest growth. In Omron's case, we were lucky enough to pick up information concerning the automation market early on and, believing firmly in its future, to begin exploiting it, thus positioning ourselves firmly in a high-growth market. This happy combination of events was directly responsible for the solid growth that Omron experienced thereafter.

Yet the cultivation of a new market is no simple thing. Ever since the Meiji Restoration of 1868, Japanese manufacturers had been able to catch up with and even overtake the developed nations of the West by simply getting samples of the products available in the West, improving on them, and bringing the new versions onto the market. Nowadays that practice is called "copycat production." A graphic example is the Model Z microswitch that our company developed — that is, copied — at the request of the Air Force during the Pacific War.

When the automation market was first opened up, however, there simply weren't any samples available for copying.

The fact is that every piece of automation-related control equipment that is manufactured and sold by Omron — switches, relays, timers and the like — is developed in-house.

For new development you need to search out development projects. We directed our salesmen to sniff out any and all things our customers required, which is to say, the needs of society. "An Omron salesman doesn't merely sell products," we told them. "The other half of the job is to identify the needs for which the next product will be developed."

Society's needs, after all, constitute opportunities to develop the next product or technology or system. The objective is to foresee as many of those needs as possible, and to be the first to develop the technology, products, and systems to satisfy those needs. That, in a nutshell, is my theory of social needs.

Omron has been on the front lines of research and development ever since its foundation, but it was only after this theory of social needs became clear that the entire company was placed on that footing.

I began to set out the theory of social needs in 1955, when we began development work in the automation field. I myself am an engineer with a bit of lead in my pants, and find it bothersome to concentrate on the sales side of business. Accordingly, I decided that whenever I found out about a customer's needs — "This sort of thing would be useful," or "Wouldn't something like that be possible?" — I would immediately develop the technology or the products to satisfy them.

Since technologies and products developed in this manner are born from society's needs, they more or less sell themselves. This is known as "suction sales." By comparison, when it comes to selling goods that can be found everywhere, in order to succeed, you have to resort to expensive advertising campaigns, legions of salesmen, or heavy expense accounts for wining and dining the customers, or what is known as pressure sales.

It has always been my conviction that when you start from a social need, then the suction factor will apply, and sales will occur naturally without special effort. This is the belief that molded the basic character of Omron.

PART THREE

The Interdependence of Technology and Social Needs

CHAPTER SEVEN

Secrets of Serving Tomorrow's Markets

*I*N 1952 I had two experiences that marked a turnabout in my luck. One of them was hearing Yoichi Ueno, the pioneer of efficiency studies in Japan, speak about automation. The other was learning from Dr. Katsuzo Nishi, the previously mentioned founder of the Nishi medical system, about the new science of cybernetics.

Dr. Ueno and I were both members of a group of corporate executives in the Kyoto-Osaka-Kobe area, called the Gleaners Club, who met monthly to hear about diverse topics from knowledgeable people in the Kansai region. Dr. Ueno spoke to us about automation one day.

During the war, he told us, there was in America "an automated factory" without a single human operator. The materials were fed in, and out came splendid products. For the production of the future, Dr. Ueno concluded, we have to start planning for automated factories.

At that time, automation was virtually unknown in Japan, and this information was a revelation to us. Personally, I was instantly fascinated by this news of automation. I kept turning it over in my mind, thinking that this might well be the most promising market of the future. Eventually, I began to think about the new control equipment that would be used for automation, and those thoughts set me tinkering. I had improved the microswitch we had originally created in 1943, and developed new magnetic relays, timer relays, and the like, and showed the prototypes around to see what people thought of them. The favorable responses I received helped me make up my mind, in 1955, to enter the automation market.

With that, my company's operations, which since its founding in 1933 had been limited to making protective relays, expanded into another dimension. We rushed ahead of other firms into the then nonexistent Japanese market for automation control equipment, and established a mass-production organization. As a result, for several years Omron was the only company serving that market, and that laid the foundation for the company's current prosperity. Now, 35 years later, it is clear that the decision to launch into the automation market was the turning point for Omron.

Early History of Omron

When I look back on the words of Professor Ueno, I realize the tremendous relevance they had to me, and how lucky I was to hear them. Indeed, his words were what made it possible for us to set about exploiting the automation market.

Perhaps these words held so much meaning for me because just at that time I was intently seeking new directions for my company.

On May 10, 1933, at Higashi Noda in Osaka, I had founded Japan's first company to specialize exclusively in the manufacture of relays. Performance steadily increased after 1937, when we moved into a new factory at Nozato, near the Tsukamoto station of the national railway, and the number of employees grew to about 250. Then on March 6, 1945, during the major air raid on Osaka, seven firebombs turned the factory to ruins. As it happened, the year before the company had assumed title to the unused Arakan Productions movie lot in the Omuro district in Kyoto, and we had begun converting it into a factory to which we could evacuate our operations. After the bombing we worked furiously to finish it, and then on the day it became sufficiently usable to move into, the war ended. (The site was later used to build the current head office, and the name of the area, Omuro, inspired the new corporate name, Omron, which was adopted in 1958.)

⁻Industry was in such a state of ruin after the war that there was absolutely no demand for production components like relays. Although the company was converted from a private holding into a joint-stock corporation in 1948, economic stagnation continued, and by 1950 the total number of employees had shrunk to thirty-three, including myself. That was the turning point. The Japanese economy at last started down the road to recovery, and as demand for electrical equipment began to reappear, it seemed that the company would be able to support the thirty-three of us. At that point I began to think seriously about how to revive the Tateisi Electric Company.

No matter how I looked at it, however, I couldn't see how we could return to the wartime operations level of 250 employees by making only our previous products. I therefore began groping around for some market that could open up dreams for many new products. It was against such a background that I heard Professor Ueno's talk and the door to automation swung open.

The Impact of Cybernetics

During that same year, 1952, I heard Dr. Nishi speak of the new science of cybernetics, which he said was all the rage in America. He went on to tell us how cybernetics had been expounded in a series of lectures by Norbert Weiner at the Massachusetts Institute of Technology during 1948 and that Dr. Weiner had written a book that gave a complete, detailed explanation.

When this book was first published, it came as a great shock to the American labor unions. They envisioned a gloomy scenario in which the new science would be fully adopted, human beings would no longer be needed at the workplace, and the whole workforce would lose their jobs. In fact, the unions were so violently opposed to a reprinting of the book that it became impossible to put out new editions, and that made it very hard to come by in Japan. Therefore, about one hundred interested people got together and produced a pirate edition by mimeograph. Dr. Nishi quoted from a copy of this mimeographed pirate edition.

The book, *Cybernetics: Control and Communication in Animals and Machines*, could not be fully comprehended without mastery of a dozen or so different academic disciplines, from mathematics, physics, and chemistry to electronics, telecommunications, and even psychology. It concerned what might be called the science of control (specifically, human control functions and the design of mechanical and electronic systems to replace them), and it represented a fundamental shift in thinking. Indeed, Dr. Weiner was among the first to realize that the underpinnings of the coming wave of control engineering could not be grasped without seeking aid from such traditionally unrelated areas as biology and psychology.

This points up the truism that no matter what great advancements may be achieved in science and technology, it is always people who will put them to use. Even the most elegant system will not hold up if the human link is removed. In this idea we perceive the essential dignity of man as compared with machines.

It is that concept which gave rise to Dr. Weiner's thesis that the most humane way to treat people is to place them in only those jobs from which the human element cannot be eliminated, while leaving to machines all of those tasks that can be mechanically performed. That is, anything that can be done mechanically should be left entirely to machines, while people perform those tasks that require thinking or creativity. This is the most humanistic approach to work that I can think of.

While few ventured to point out the absolute absurdity of the idea that human beings would be completely eliminated, it was not long before the theories of cybernetics were applied to a new wave of technology called cybernation (the use of computers to regulate automatic processes). In this way automatic control technology made great strides. To put it more concretely, adding a feedback function to automatic control technology is automation, and combining computers with automation is cybernetics. Omron independently developed cybernation as an outgrowth of our work on a coupon vending machine in 1963 — a major innovation for us. That independently achieved application of computers to automation was to be the driving force of the company's later development.

At any rate, 1952 stands out as a critical year for me because that was when both of the concepts that were to be so fateful for Omron — automation and cybernetics — first came to my attention. Naturally, I retain a debt of heartfelt thanks to the two teachers who brought those words to my ears (Figure 8).

Figure 8. History of Omron Tateisi Electronics Co.

1900 Kazuma Tateisi (Founder and Chairman of the Board) born in Kumamoto

1908 K. Tateisi's father passed away on March 26 of an illness when Tateisi was seven years old

1921 K. Tateisi graduated from Kumamoto High School of Technology (presently Kumamoto University), majoring in electro-chemistry
K. Tateisi served as an electric engineer in the Civil Engineering Section of Hyogo Prefecture Government

1922 K. Tateisi joined Inoue Electric Manufacturing Co. in Kyoto

1930 K. Tateisi established independently a business named Saikosha in Kyoto and started production and sales of a home pants press

1931 Timer for X-ray pictures developed

1933 K. Tateisi concluded OEM contract for timer with Dainihon X-ray Inc., in Osaka

K. Tateisi established, on May 10, the company of Tateisi Electric Manufacturing Co., located at 21, 5-chome, Higashi Noda, Miyakojima-ku, Osaka City, and started business with two employees

1934 Induction type protective relay developed

1935 Business reorganized to specialize in the production of electromagnetic relays

1936 New factory opened, and office moved to 81, Nozato-cho, Nishiyodogawa-ku, Osaka City

1937 Thesis by K. Tateisi titled, "Thermionic Tube Overload Relay" published in the special May issue of OHM, a monthly publication on electricity

1940 New annex to the factory built
AV type magnetic relay developed

1941 Internal development of precision-switches started

1942 K. Tateisi coordinated factory for Mitsubishi Electric Corporation

1943 Precision-switches produced internally

1944 Kyoto 2nd Studio of Shochiku Cinema Corp. purchased and remodelled to Kyoto Branch Factory (the present location of the Head Office)

1945 Both Tokyo Office and Osaka Main Factory destroyed by fire in air raids

Head Office moved to Kyoto Branch Factory at the end of the war

Business reorganized by production and sales of home heating appliances

Adjustable heating device developed

1946 Hair iron for women, Date (Jujube) Type Quality Electric Lighter, Electric Long-Life Matches, and the Z-5 Type Precision-Switch developed

"OMRON" trademark first used

1947 Current limiter developed
Company appointed as a designated manufacturer by the government
Pressure switch developed

1948 Tateisi Electronics Co. founded, capitalized with ¥ 2 million

1949 Production of current limiter stopped, subject to the order effected by Dodge-line
Number of employees reduced in three steps

1950 Business resumed with 33 members, including the President
Tokyo Office reestablished
Mrs. Tateisi deceased
Worst annual sales record posted, dropping to merely 57 percent of the preceding year

1951 Part of the factory rented to a motion picture company as studio until 1952
Office established in Osaka

1952 Information obtained from Mr. Yoichi Ueno on the automation system and from Mr. Katsuzo Nishi on Cybernetics which were decisive factors for the future of the business

1953 Successful reestablishment of the company declared at the 20th anniversary celebration
President K. Tateisi visited United States for the first time to inspect small and medium-sized electric factories. When he returned from the trip, he instructed the company to develop the components for automation systems

1954 President K. Tateisi honored with a Blue Ribbon Medal for the service rendered by his inventions

1955 To effect decentralized management in the company business, Tateisi Electronics Sales Co. and Tateisi Electronics R&D Laboratory established
Also, for the "producer system," Saikyo Electronics Manufacturing founded as the first producer company (P)

1956 President K. Tateisi visited Europe for the first time as a member of a group of representatives from the Japan United Nations Bureau

The Precision-Switch approved for MIL Specifications and accepted by the Japanese Defense Agency

1957 Tokyo Office promoted to the Tokyo Branch Office

First athletic meet held for all Tateisi employees at the site of the Main Office on sports ground prepared by employees

The company's annual motto selected and announced as "quality first"

"Enshukah" and "Kaian" buildings completed in commemoration of the 20th anniversary of the business

1958 "OMRON" registered as trademark

Tateisi Electronics R&D Laboratory consolidated

1959 Non-contact proximity switch successfully developed

New building of Central R&D Laboratory completed

1960 Tateisi Electronics Technical Seminar started

"Tateisi Denki Mutsumikai" established as an internal organization for all Tateisi entities

1961 Medical application business entered with development of a stress meter

Basic model precision switch accepted by JIS Specifications

1962 Company stocks offered to the public

A P system for the managing directorship effected

Trial production of Model TCS coin selector completed

1963 Long term export contract signed for the midget-type Magnetic Relay with Key Switch Corp. U.K.

Automatic Vending Machine and Bank Notes and Coin Exchange Machines developed

Participated in Tokyo International Trade Exhibition

Representative office opened in New York

Dr. Hans Selye (world-renowned authority on stress management) invited to Japan; signed a contract for cooperative research on health engineering

1964 Neo-producer system (Neo-P) No. 1 named Iida Tateisi Electronics founded in Iida City

First success in the world made of practical experiment with automatically operated electronic traffic signals using a self-sensing system (intersection traffic control system)

1965 Consolidation of all Tateisi business entities (Neo-P excluded) completed

Multi-function electronic automatic ticket vending machine developed

An automatic sensing-type, electronically controlled traffic signal erected at No. 14 Intersection in Naniwa-suji, Osaka City, which was successful in controlling the traffic flow on the roads

Automatic vending machine to be used with a card system demonstrated jointly with Automatic Canteen of U.S., in New York

Automated diagnostic apparatus based on the oriental medical physiotherapy system developed

1966 Automated season ticket issuing machine developed

Erected, at 34 Intersection located in Nihonbashi and Ginza Wards, a wide range of automatically controlled electronic traffic signals

Electronic traffic control system completed

1967 First unmanned railway station built and operated at the Kitasenri Station of Hankyu Railways

First automated cancer cell detecting apparatus in the world developed

1968 Head Office building completed in commemoration of the company's 35th anniversary

Electric artificial limb for handicapped (Thalidomide) children developed

1969 Smallest electronic desk top calculator, "Calculet 1200," developed

Checking machine for depositor's card developed

Automatic off-line cash dispenser developed

1970 2.5 million stock shares of the European Deposit Receipt (EDR) issued

SINIC theory presented at the International Future Research Conference held in Kyoto

K. Tateisi honored with a doctorate in medical science for the research done in developing the electric artificial limb

K. Tateisi decorated with the Order of the Rising Sun, Third Class, with Star and Ribbon

1971   First on-line cash dispenser in the world successfully
        developed and operated at the Mitsubishi Bank, Ltd.,
        Head Office

        First overseas production company (WP), The Omron
        de Baja California, established in Mexico

        Joint business venture, Thorn-Omron Ltd., established
        in U.K.

1972   Omron Taiyo Electronics, a factory established for the
        handicapped (Mini-P No 1), opened in Beppu City

        POS system submitted to Kagoshima Credit Sales

1973   Omron Technical Fair (OTF) held in commemoration of the
        company's 40th anniversary, using the Shin Sakura Maru
        (GT 13,000) for display and opened to the public at 12 ports
        around Japan

1974   Color liquid crystal display for electronic calculators
        developed for the first time in the world

1975   The Banking and Retail Systems Production Factory
        designated by Nippon Telegraph and Telephone Public
        Corporation as its approved factory

        The Crown Prince and Princess visited Omron Taiyo
        Electronics

1976   Consultant agreement signed with U.S. McKinsey &
        Company Inc., Japan Branch

        MIC, a committee for management improvement, organized

        Reorganization of the company effected

        Company stock nominated as a special issue at Osaka
        Securities Exchange

        Women's Handball Team won four titles in national sports
        competition

1977   Subsidiaries in the U.S. and their accrued losses written off
        as a special loss

        Computerized blood cell analyzer developed, the first such
        system made in Japan

1978   Cooperative sales agreement signed with SCI and Motorola
        of U.S. and Telemechanics of France

1979   Convertible bond amounting to 50 million in Deutschemark
        issued

Annual sales of ¥ 10.11 billion achieved independently by Omron Tateisi Electronics Co.

Kazuma Tateisi appointed to the position of Chairman of the Board and Takao Tateisi to President

An export agreement with Korea on the ticket vending machine signed

A midget timepiece with the liquid crystal digital system announced

1980   500 billion in sales set as the target for the company by the end of eighties

A trade agreement on technological application in the control device signed with Yantzu Electrical Works in Shanghai, the People's Republic of China

1981   Chairman K. Tateisi decorated with the Second of the Sacred Treasure

The production of 10,000 units of CDs and ATMs achieved (the first in the world)

The free use of patents realized

1982   Building of Keishinkan, the Omron Training Center, completed

Complete order received for traffic control systems to be built in Taiwan

Practical participation in the development of optical communications system announced

1983   An "order for emergency counter measures against large-scale business depressions" made

Chairman K. Tateisi criticized the company as being seriously inflicted by big business syndrome

A reformation of the business entity and an extensive reorganization to be made in the system announced

A company memorial service for deceased employees held and a memorial monument to honor them erected

A scholarship for the children of deceased employees of Omron organized

An order received for the traffic control system for Pusan City in S. Korea

Celebration of the company's fiftieth anniversary held at each of the business entities

1984 A contract signed to export, in knocked-down parts, kits of health machines to the People's Republic of China

Warrant bond in $ for $30 million issued in U.S. and a ¥7 billion converted bond issued in Japan

A project to establish a Tokyo Telecommunications Laboratory announced

1987 Yoshio Tateisi appointed President of Omron Tateisi Electronics Co.

Vital Points of Long-Range Planning

It was in the mid-1950s, as I began to think in terms of creating and serving the large new market of automation equipment, that I began to take long-range planning seriously. Later, as a result of Professor Drucker's first visit to Japan in 1959, there was a boom in the study of American-style management techniques, and it became fashionable for companies to prepare long-range plans. That was when we decided that Omron needed a five-year plan. Covering the years from 1960 to 1964, the first plan set a final sales target of ¥10 billion (about $28 million). Compared to the 1959 net sales total of ¥1.2 billion, we were predicting roughly tenfold growth. In fact, net sales had already grown tenfold between 1954 and 1959, from ¥0.12 billion to ¥1.2 billion, and we thought we could achieve a similar rate of growth in the next five-year period.

There were two key factors behind the goals we set in the plan. One was our realization that if we had grown tenfold from 1954 to 1959, it was largely because the automation market itself had grown spectacularly. The question was whether the market would continue to expand at the same pace for the ensuing five years. I had no doubt about the answer. I was firmly convinced that automation was the lever of the second industrial revolution. It was widely believed at that time that the true industrial shift would be an energy revolution brought on by atomic power; but while we were waiting for big news in that area the technological innovation known as automation was making real progress. I was betting on automation as the leading player in the first phase of the revolution. I also noticed that the first industrial revolution took about fifty years to reach fruition, and concluded that the second would cover a similar timespan. Taking 1950 as year one for Japanese automation, the revolution would continue until the turn of the century, the year 2000. Therefore, we based our five-year plan on the assumption that expansion of the automation market would continue for some 50 years.

It was just at that time that Matsushita Electric (best known for its National and Panasonic brands of products) became the first of the second wave of makers to begin microswitch production. They were four years behind Omron. The general manager in charge of the effort at Matsushita visited me at my home one day, and politely told me that they were going to start making microswitches. Imagine! The competitor came with a straight face to the president of the original maker and threw down the gauntlet! I had mixed feelings, but after a little thought, I decided it was a blessing. Matsushita had done me the favor of endorsing my conviction of five years earlier, that the automation market was promising enough to warrant a bold venture effort. For a reputable maker like Matsushita to be eyeing the potential of someone else's product line, and jumping into the field in the wake of a relatively unknown medium-sized firm, was an unmistakable sign that they had high expectations for the automation market. In the end, this interlude served to support our prediction that automation had a bright future.

Because of the recession of 1961-62, we reached the 10-billion mark two years late, in 1966. Meanwhile, in 1965 we had embarked on our next five-year plan. As it happened, in 1966 the Japanese government announced the Economic and Social Development Plan, which called for a 12.5 percent rate of annual growth in the gross national product for the period from 1967 through 1971. In order to fall in line with that schedule, we prepared a revised third five-year plan, to take effect from 1967. At that point I began thinking in terms of a coefficient of elasticity. I compared Omron's growth rate over the previous five years with that of the national rate, obtaining a coefficient of 3.5. I then multiplied that figure by the projected national growth rate, 12.5 percent, to predict the average annual rate of growth that the company could expect. Adding a margin for extra increases in export markets, we set ¥45 billion as a realistic goal for the 1971 sales total.

The depreciation of the dollar in August 1971 sharply affected our business results, making our total sales for the year ¥40.1 billion, or only 90 percent of the target. It didn't take long for our plans to be vindicated, however, for sales in 1972 reached ¥51.5 billion.

Since that time all our long-range planning has been done in the same general manner. Is this method guaranteed to achieve results in the company? I can't say that I have no doubts whatsoever, but of one thing I am sure, and that is that the process works to raise company morale. Once the plan is articulated, everyone picks up the spirit.

Sixty Percent of Sales Consist of New Products

The second big factor influencing our planning was the realization that some 60 percent of net sales in 1959 had been generated by products that we had developed during the previous five years. The conclusion was inescapable: our growth had resulted from our heavy commitment to research and development.

In that case, it seemed that a necessary condition for reaching the sales target of ¥10 billion would be sufficient R & D strength to generate the new products that could bring in ¥6 billion per year by 1964. That could never have been accomplished by the small-scale development department of our existing research section in the 1950s. Realizing that a serious R & D lab was absolutely necessary, I resolved to build the Central R & D Laboratory, which was completed in 1960.

CHAPTER EIGHT

A Unique R & D System

I N 1955, Omron launched full-scale business activities for the making of automation equipment. Since that venture was the move that caused the company to grow to its present scale, I have come to call it "automation year one."

When we actually began doing business, we ran into more trouble than we had counted on. As I have said, there was no such thing as an automation market in Japan at that time, and the products began to take shape only after the sales representatives had gone around to assess the demands of potential customers (the social needs). That was indeed a difficult job. The R & D staff would develop products to satisfy the needs that we had identified, and from there the actual production and sales would begin.

Nevertheless, as a result of doing business in that way, the company's sales grew from ¥240 million in 1955 to ¥2.3 billion in 1960 — a tenfold increase in five years. By then I was saying to myself, "We have found the perfect market."

In the midst of that difficult but successful period, I decided in 1959 to establish a new R & D laboratory. My reasoning was that the market would expand at the same rate at which we were able to increase our R & D strength. At first I calculated an investment of no more than twenty or thirty million yen (about $50,000-$80,000), which at the time was still quite a bit of money. Then the Electronics Industry Promotion Law was enacted, and the Electronics Industry Federation was established, as a result of which our company's mainstay product line, microswitches, came to be used in more and more electronic devices. As Japan's quasi-public development bank began financing the makers of electronic equipment, it appeared probable that we could obtain considerable funding.

In the end, I approached the development bank with a request for ¥50 million, planning to match that with a like amount from our own resources. From that moment, there was no turning back. We proceeded to modify our plans in order to spend ¥100 million (about $300,000) on the construction of a research center. Land was purchased in Nagaoka, just south of the city of Kyoto, and the building was completed in October 1960.

After starting construction, we realized that various world-class equipment should be acquired, including measuring and testing apparatus and calibration devices. The upshot was that we grossly exceeded our budget. By the time it was finished, we had spent a total of ¥280 million (about $780,000). The company's paid-up capital in 1959 amounted to ¥70 million; we had thrown precisely four times that sum into the research laboratory! People began whispering about "the technician-president's new toy," but I didn't let them bother me, for in making the original decision I had been fully aware that I was taking a very big risk.

As it turned out, the completed Central Research and Development Laboratory soon contributed to the commercialization of many products that met diverse social needs, and became the driving force for Omron's ongoing development.

The Importance of Project Screening: From Ideas to Products

From the beginning, Omron has carried out its research and development with the intent to make products that serve social needs, and we have no intention of altering this policy.

Catching on to social needs before others do means picking up information quickly, and to do this one must use the entire company as a set of antennae. The executive himself will often collect information concerning certain systems or major projects, but the simplest path to information about the company's current products is through the sales network. Salespeople must sell products, of course, but at Omron their job doesn't end there. They also carry out the important responsibility of collecting information from product users so that trends in social needs can be ascertained.

How should the information be collected and recorded in practical terms? Because gathering and communicating customer feedback is so vital to our product development strategy, we have devised a simple system for salespeople to collect, record, and communicate this information effectively.

It is troublesome for salespeople to write reports after they return to the office. Instead, we ask the sales force to carry writing paper with them in the field, to make memos on the spot whenever they pick up anything of interest. They then circulate these notes on their return to the office.

This grassroots marketing research method turns up an endless variety of miscellany, which is collated and passed along to the planning sections of the respective divisions for screening.

Another important step in promoting the creation of products that serve social needs is the product evaluation meeting. At Omron, it is held once a month and is attended by the division managers. At a single meeting perhaps ten or twenty projects will be proposed. The division managers immediately screen each idea by evaluating its essentials.

Although I am not an official member, I attend the product meetings as an observer and occasionally offer an opinion. If the group determines that a certain theme is worthy of becoming a development project, then the development division is ordered to proceed.

This kind of procedure is critical to the R & D process. We used to include middle managers in the product meetings, but their presence slowed down the decision-making process. This indecisiveness stemmed from the useless tendency to place the burden for failures on the middle managers. A middle manager's role in a failure ultimately becomes the responsibility of the senior manager. Thus it became obvious that we should leave the responsibility at the top from the beginning. Once it became clear that the product evaluation meeting was the responsibility of senior managers, then the screening and transition to the development stage proceeded swiftly.

The products discussed at a product evaluation meeting are not based exclusively on information obtained by executives or sales personnel. Sometimes the development staff independently comes up with ideas. Research on one theme may lead to an unexpected discovery. When ideas generated in that manner reach the product evaluation stage, we call them the "eager agenda."

Executives, then, make the final decisions on important projects, and thereby assume responsibility for any failures. It is, therefore, incumbent upon them to understand the technology. In this era of technological innovation, while an executive need not actually be a technician, he at least must be able to evaluate new technology.

Three-Stage System of Product Development

When the development department receives an order to move forward on a particular project, they hold crucial meetings to initiate the three stages of the development process. Each is chaired by the department manager; the other members include the various supervisory staff of the sales and production departments who are concerned with the project.

Stage 1 begins with the design evaluation meeting. The project proceeds to stage 2, with the startup review meeting, and then to stage 3, the production review meeting. If the new product is a component for a certain machine, during stage 3 the lot size will be set (it might be 1,000 or 2,000 pieces, depending on the product), then the parts are produced with temporary dies and assembled, and finally the component is tested on the main production line. Every effort is made to resolve the various problems that can be envisioned during the production start. Only after passing stage 3 does the project go to the factory, where the various mass-produced parts are assembled. If there are no problems, full-scale mass production begins.

At Omron, then, the process advances from the initial product evaluation stage through the three stages of design, startup, and production review. This series of meetings ensures a smooth transition from development to production (Figure 9).

The Open-Room R & D System

The Omron development staff utilizes an open-room pattern, in which 100 or 150 researchers work within the same four walls. This is one element of the carefully controlled Omron R & D system. It dates from 1960, when the Central Research and Development Laboratory opened.

We had spent the better part of a million dollars to build a magnificent research facility, only to find that we couldn't secure the researchers to staff it. The problem was that, back then, the venture spirit was not so widely recognized in Japan's technical circles. Our activities in electronics and automation represented a new, virtually untested field of technology, and seasoned engineers were not very responsive to our feelers. As a result, we decided to hire recent university graduates in fairly large numbers, although of course we were worried that at first they would not be able to handle the work.

After considering various alternatives, we finally settled on a plan. Even if the researchers were inexperienced, we con-

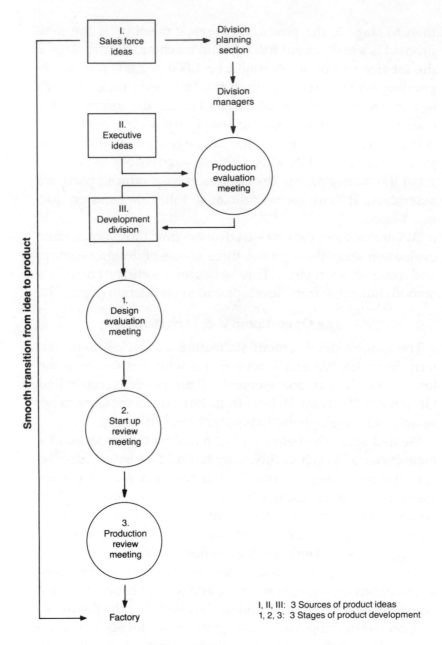

Figure 9. Product Development System

cluded, the energy of the system would draw out their potential once they were in the thick of it. We hoped to evaluate the R & D program so that it could move forward, but we didn't want it to slow down for large-scale training. Therefore, we had to devise a system that was not based solely on generating business and profit, but was also designed to allow ample returns in learning. On one level, we needed training, but more important for the long run, we thought we could build a system that would stimulate the joy of creativity and the desire to work. It was on that basis that operations at the Central Research and Development Laboratory began.

Vertical-Horizontal-Diagonal Control

Systematic control has been the distinctive feature of the Omron Central Research and Development Laboratory ever since it opened in 1960. Right from the start, we used a particular format of control called the PESIC System. PESIC stands for Projects, Elements, Services and Information Construction but we also refer to it as the vertical-horizontal-diagonal control concept.

PESIC was inspired by a set of quality control specifications issued by the United States Air Force. That document, titled MIL-Q-5923-C, was based on the concept of a structure with vertical, horizontal, and diagonal elements. It came into our hands in 1960 in connection with an order for microswitches to be used in jet fighter planes, which were about to go into production in Japan. A USAF technician explained the quality control system to us, and later, using those techniques as a foundation, we developed a system of our own, the PESIC system, that could be used in various control situations.

Today, amid the rapidly progressing microelectronics revolution, society and its institutions are confronted with innovations one after another. These various innovations are ceaselessly striking against our organizational structures. If the structure is strong, it can endure the assault, but if it has faults, then the impact may knock it down.

A business is no exception. It must invest its organizational structure with the strength to withstand the impact of innovation. Since a company is naturally constrained by various operational and financial parameters, it needs to utilize its limited resources of personnel and equipment in the most efficient way possible. In the case of Omron, the PESIC system provided a highly efficient organizational concept for steering the company through the era of increasing innovation.

The PESIC system is based on an understanding of the relative strengths of three types of structures:

1. Vertical elements: a structure consisting only of pillars
2. Vertical and horizontal elements: a structure consisting of a combination of pillars and crossbeams
3. Vertical, horizontal, and diagonal elements: a structure consisting of pillars and crossbeams as well as diagonal braces

If we assign a value of 1 to the vertical-horizonal-diagonal structure, then the vertical-horizontal structure has a strength of $3/4$, and the unreinforced vertical structure has an extremely low strength of $1/30$.

Obviously, the triaxial arrangement has the most strength and allows for the most efficient structural systems. Its efficiency is achieved through the allocation of strength according to the dynamic relationships of the vertical, horizontal, and diagonal elements.

The PESIC system is the means of applying that theoretical framework to the organization of a company. It is extremely efficient as both an organizational configuration and as a means of control.

To explain the PESIC system in concrete terms, the Omron R & D control structure consists of the principles outlined below. The initials *P, E,* and *SI,* respectively, correspond to the vertical, horizontal, and diagonal elements outlined above.

P stands for projects, products, or purpose. It is the objective, the central current of the activities, and it is assigned the structural role of the vertical element. For a manufacturing company, this element is classified by product.

E means elements or engineering. Its role is to give form to the *P* components, and thus it is the horizontal element. In a manufacturing company it is classified by technology, by material, and by scientific field.

S is for services or supports. Supplementing the crossframe of *P* and *E,* it is a diagonal element of the structure. It includes the mechanical and managerial spheres and the miscellaneous technologies that back up the products, engineering, or information.

I means information, ideas, investigation, or invention. This is another supplementary, diagonal element. It is the semi-technical sphere that includes software and planning relevant to the *P* and *E* elements, and it may overlap the *S* category.

The Laboratory Control System

Our first application of the PESIC system was to the organization and control methods of our R & D program beginning in 1960.

At first we structured the laboratories in the typical way, to correspond directly to product lines. In those days Omron's main products were microswitches, magnet relays, timer relays, and the recently developed contactless proximity switch, and so separate labs were laid out for each of those areas. This, of course, is vertical, P (project)-based control.

Soon enough, we found that the various laboratories were encountering similar problems. There was frequent duplication of work on parts that could be used in all types of products. To eliminate the wasted effort, we created a horizontal structure specializing in generic elements such as springs, electromagnets, contactless switches, permanent magnets, and transistor circuits. This was horizontal, E (element)-based control (Figure 10).

Next, we carried out some work sampling to find out how much of the researcher's time was being spent on fundamental research. The results were surprising. We defined three categories of technicians, according to how advanced their research projects were, and found that only 20 percent were in the highest category. It is probably true at any company — especially, perhaps, at Japanese companies — that the more

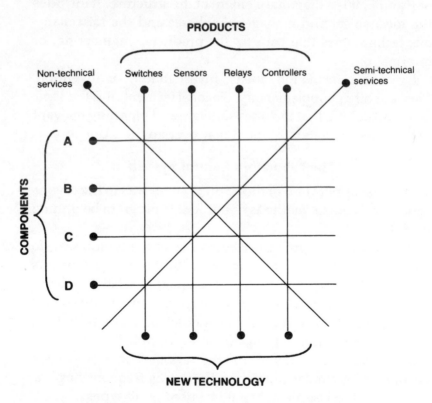

Figure 10. PESIC System Applied to the R & D Structure

senior the researcher, the more miscellaneous, nonresearch duties pile up. They attend a great many meetings of professional organizations and committees, receive many guests, and spend considerable time communicating with people outside the company. It stands to reason that if researchers can be relieved of these numerous chores, they will have more time to devote to actual research and development.

Therefore, we supplemented the vertical-horizontal control with a diagonal, S (service) component. The basic need was for office services, and we met it by assigning permanent secretaries to each of the laboratory heads. Until that time, even though these researchers were senior managers, few had private secretaries. In addition to the secretaries who were put in charge of miscellaneous tasks, a special office service center was set up to serve the basic needs of the whole R & D division. Beyond the office level, we created a special center for technical information services (the I-component), which collected and managed a variety of data in order to serve as a ready reference facility. This is the diagonal, support axis that runs perpendicular to that of the office services (Figure 10).

Later, we were able to identify seven concrete advantages of the vertical-horizontal-diagonal R & D configuration:

1. No duplication of operations among various laboratories
2. Easier recognition of shortcomings to be rectified
3. Increased specialization and more advanced results
4. Standardization easily achieved
5. Organizational flexibility to set up specialist task forces for specific objectives
6. Optimal use of individual talents, and more job enthusiasm
7. Higher efficiency

Decentralized Restructuring with the PESIC System

As a company's scale of operations grows, the president will lose the ability to singlehandedly oversee everything. Speaking from my own experience, the president will still be able to closely handle the operations of a company with 50 employees, but when the total reaches 100, hands-on management is beyond one person's capability. Since I am an engineer and high finance has never been my forte, the first person I brought in as a partner was an accountant. The growing sales force also complicated management. When we grew to a total of about 100 employees, a thorough reorganization became necessary.

There are various theories of corporate structure, but to my mind the most important is the decentralization of management. This idea began to spread in Japan in about 1959 as a result of the first visits to Japan by the American management specialist, Professor Peter F. Drucker. At Omron, our own experience had already made us keenly aware of the need to decentralize. We initiated our unique Producer System in 1955. This is based on the same principles of decentralization that Drucker advocated in Japan a few years later.

The divisional form of decentralization became quite popular around 1960. The basic idea, of course, is that when a company has many types of products and markets, control is virtually impossible without the provision of some divisional independence. Unfortunately, there are a surprising number of companies where divisional organization has been poorly implemented. I have seen cases, in which a company with several different products aimed at the same market makes the mistake of setting up a division for each *product*. One division per *market* is an axiom in decentralization.

It was not until 1970 that Omron began using a market-based divisional structure, and the corporate reorganization that we carried out at that time was based on the PESIC system. Applied to corporate structure, the PESIC system consists of product divisions as the vertical members and headquarters' staff as the horizontal members, with the areas of functional overlap between divisions and headquarters as the diagonal members (Figure 11).

The vertical component is line operations, and thus naturally the division. In the case of the horizontal component, or headquarters, the job is functionally comparable to research and development. The division manager must be informed and competent in each of the key functions connected with the division, but in actual practice, his background will usually be strongest in a particular area, perhaps production or

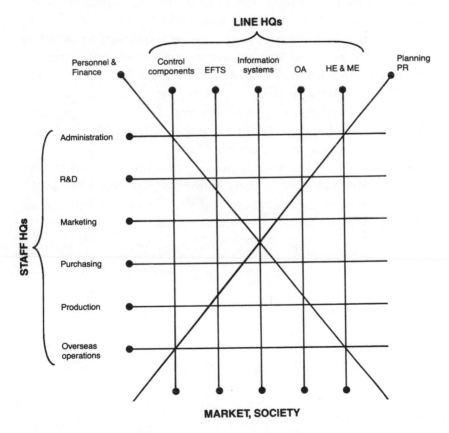

Figure 11. PESIC System Applied to the Corporate Management Structure

sales. Since it is unreasonable to expect him to be expert in every aspect of the division's business, the headquarters' staff covers whichever functions the various divisions may require.

The headquarters is a technostructure, a group of knowledgeable specialists who act as consultants, advisers, and coordinators. Rather than serving as the command authority of a division, the headquarters maintains instructional or advising authority. Although instructions and advice are necessarily somewhat weaker than orders, we have developed a general understanding that advice from headquarters is to be taken, as well as given, very seriously.

We established separate corporate headquarters for administration, human relations, marketing, research and development, production, purchasing, and overseas activities. As for the diagonal elements of the structure, we set up headquarters to handle functions such as accounting, finance, and personnel on the one hand, with others on the opposite diagonal axis covering planning and public relations.

The R & D system and corporate structure outlined above were modified as the company continued to develop, so as to match changing circumstances and above all to erect the most suitable systems for meeting social needs.

CHAPTER NINE

First Era of Growth

O N the basis of the theory of social needs, the Omron sales force began making energetic efforts to grasp actual demands. Requests came into my hands one after another, and among them was one that was quite novel and, when we began to think about it, quite difficult to realize. Somebody asked, "How about making your switches so that they will last about a thousand times longer?"

Now, a switch had two electrical contacts, the operating principle being that when it came into physical contact with some object, the current would flow, and when it lost contact, the current would cease. Each time the current was cut, an electric arc was generated, causing wear on the contact. At the time the longest service life for a switch was about 10,000 on/off cycles, after which it was completely worn out.

Along with advances in automation, however, the frequency of switch cycles was increasing exponentially; as a result, switches with a service life of about 10,000 cycles were used up in just one week. Each time that happened, the machinery had to be shut off to change the switch, and the downtime represented a significant loss in productivity. It was not surprising, then, that customers wanted to extend the service life of the switches by several orders of magnitude — to about 100 million on/off cycles.

No matter how much ingenuity was applied, that long a life was something that simply couldn't be achieved with the existing structure and parts. At this point I made an about-face in the conception of the switch. "In the first place," I realized, "the reason the service life is so short is that the switch has contacts. To make it last longer, you have to get rid of the contacts."

Then another idea came along. In August 1955, Sony had succeeded in developing the world's first transistor radio. I attended the gala demonstration and sale that was held for the new product at the Hankyu Department Store in Osaka. I bought one for myself on the spot, and I got into the habit of listening to it at home before I went to sleep. One night, I had a flash of inspiration: if the right sort of transistorized circuit were devised, it should be possible to make a switch with no contacts.

For a little while, I kept the idea to myself. Then on May 10, 1958, at the ceremony marking the 25th anniversary of the company, I directed the research staff to come up with a transistorized, contactless switch within five years. The technicians tackled the new project immediately, and two years later, in the spring of 1960, they had successfully produced a contactless proximity switch.

This was an epoch-making device. Unlike conventional switches, which had to be brought by some external force into direct contact with an object, the new switch could generate a current when it simply came near a metal object, and the current would stop when the switch was moved away from the metal. For the first time, in the field of control technology at least, it was shown that electronics could lead to genuine technological innovation. Wasting no time, I took it to an international trade show that spring, and the debut of the "dream switch" was a sensation. Another year or two passed before

Westinghouse and General Electric developed contactless switches.

Not only did the proximity switch, by virtue of its lack of contacts, have the advantage of a semi-permanent service life, it also had a conspicuously faster response time. While a contact-type switch could complete 200 or 300 on/off circuits per minute, with a contactless switch the frequency shot up to several thousand per minute.

That fall, with what seemed like perfect timing, the Central Research and Development Laboratory was completed, and shortly thereafter a torrent of new developments and applications for contactless switches was issuing from it.

After developing the contactless switch, we developed contactless relays and contactless timers, and in 1961 Omron began marketing automatic equipment containing combinations of various control devices that were based on contactless elements (Figure 12).

Figure 12. History of Omron Product Development from 1955 to 1985

1955 Production of electromagnetic relays begun
Improvement of timer and microswitch products

1956 Microswitches receive MIL rating from US Air Force

1958 Production of control panels begun

1960 World's first solid-state proximity switch developed

1961 Contactless relay developed
Microswitches receive UL and JIS certifications

1962 Entered medical treatment field with development of Stressmeter
Production of electronic control panels begun, using proximity switch and contactless relay technologies

1963 Development of automatic vending machine with electronic calculation and changemaking functions
Automatic flaw detector developed

1964 Electronic traffic signal developed

1965 Development of automatic diagnostic equipment for Oriental physiotherapy
Development and export of vending machine accepting credit cards

1966 Automatic parking fee collection system developed
On-line traffic control system installed in the Ginza

1967 World's first large unmanned railway station created in Osaka
Cancer cell diagnostic system developed

1968 Electric artificial limbs developed
Development of Cybaron electronic control system for standard production applications

1969 Development of world's smallest electronic calculator (12-digit, single-memory)
World's first depositor ID card verification system developed
Expressway traffic control system developed
Japan's first automatic cash dispenser developed
Development of group-control system for ticket vending machines

1971 Invention of Multiechelon Method for computerized traffic control systems
Cash depositing machine developed
Marketing of popularly-priced (¥ 40,000) electronic calculators
Fully automatic parking fee collection system developed

1972 Japan's first POS system developed and installed
Electronic sphygmomanometer developed

1973 Hydraulic-clutch cash register developed
SYSMAC programmable controller developed
Completion of Japan's largest traffic control system in Osaka

Entered optical semiconductor field with series linkage of 60 units using 8 new elements

1974 Air ticket vending machine developed

Electronic cash register marketed

Multiobjective card POS system developed

1975 Minibank system developed

Microcontroller and process module developed

1976 Development of linked multifunction ticket vending machines accepting banknotes

1977 MICROX automated blood cell analyzer developed

1978 Automatic cash deposit/withdrawal machine (ATM) developed

Development of F-system 2-person checkout terminals

Optical switch and microswitch awarded gold medals at expositions in Leipzig and Hanover

1979 Omron wins New Technology Award of Japan Medical Electronics Association for MICROX development

Development of ECR incorporating dot printer and display tube

Postal savings cash dispenser developed

1980 Bicycle parking system developed

Microcontroller-equipped electronic thermometer developed

1981 Total ATM/CD production reaches 10,000

1982 PBX marketing begun as agent for Rolm Co. of US

Credit card authorization terminal developed

Micom-Base Ginza personal computer hardware/software sales and consulting center opened in Tokyo

1983 Popularly priced electronic thermometer marketed

Thick-film humidity sensor and color discrimination element developed

Development of fiber-optic system with single-track, multidirectional transmission module

Marketing of PC-multihost-firm banking system with intracompany direct cash dispensing function

SYSMAC C series fiber-optic programmable controllers
marketed

Installation of automatic hotel reception/checkout system

Marketing of multiunit POS terminals

Marketing of various connectors and mechatronic
components

1984 Single-board 8-bit factory computer marketed

Lactate analyzer marketed

14 new electronic sensors marketed simultaneously

Marketing of advanced factory computer and color graphics
terminal

Marketing of software development system for use with
microcontroller-equipped components

Installation of bank POS terminal for electronic settlement

Videotex shopping terminals installed at Tokyo railway
stations

1985 PC CAD/CAM software marketed

PC health management software marketed

Developing the Coupon Vending Machine

In 1963, soon after we began full-scale sales of the new lines
of automatic control equipment, we received a difficult challenge from the Daimaru Department Store in Kyoto. They
were planning to open a specialty restaurant in their food section on the basement level, and in order to highlight it with
something unique, they asked us to make an automatic coupon
vending machine. No simple vending machine, this was to be
capable of dispensing seven types of food coupons and handling three different coins, as well as verifying the genuineness
of the coins and making change.

The vending machines of that time in Japan were primitive
affairs that could do nothing more than issue a single 10-yen
ticket upon deposit of a single 10-yen coin. What Daimaru had

in mind would obviously be of a different order of complexity and technical advancement. That being the time of the contactless switch, however, my attitude was, "If it's harder, it's more fun." What's more, all the Omron technicians had been infected with the same spirit. Of course we accepted the challenge.

In order to satisfy the conditions laid down by Daimaru, two different technical breakthroughs were required. One was pattern recognition technology to examine and verify the coins, and the other was computation technology capable of performing addition and subtraction to at least three digits.

For the coin verification technology, it happened that we had accumulated some valuable expertise only the year before, in connection with the circulation of a large number of counterfeit 1,000-yen notes, or what was known as the "chi-37" case (after the serial numbers). This deed had sorely taxed the nation's law enforcement capabilities, and Omron had been asked by the Police Science Research Institute to develop a counterfeit banknote detection device. We had earned high praise from the institute, for we were able to deliver such a device within just eight days.

As for the computing component, we had to start from scratch, and at first the technicians were stumped. This was distressing, because without it, we would fail to satisfy the customer's needs. Furthermore, there was the problem of the man/machine interface: if the machine did not immediately confirm the amounts of money entered, the user would feel uncomfortable. That is, when a 100-yen coin is put in, the machine should display "100"; if that is followed by a 50-yen coin, the display should change to "150," and so on. Then, if the customer presses the "120" button to select a coupon of that value, the vending machine should immediately make a calculation and display "30" for the amount of change, which of course would be delivered below along with the coupon. These requirements were complex enough to require nothing less than a three-digit addition and subtraction computer.

Fortunately, by then, the Central R & D Lab was thoroughly operational and we were able independently to develop a suitable computer. We promptly produced seven automatic coupon vending machines and delivered them to Daimaru.

From Automation to Cybernation

I was a bit anxious after the machines were delivered, and occasionally I went down to the Daimaru basement to have a look. One day an old lady from the country watched another customer buy coupons and get change from the machine, whereupon she eyed it suspiciously and muttered, "I bet there's somebody in there." Seeing that, I thought, "We've really done it!" But after we filled the order for those seven machines, we weren't able to sell the product to any other department stores. We gave up, being forced to conclude that the new machine was ahead of its time.

Nevertheless, Omron reaped a wonderful benefit from the development of that machine. For we had taken our previous technology in automatic control and combined it with a computer. That is to say, through our own new technology, we had developed cybernation, thereby substantially enriching our capabilities.

Automatic control, as the name implies, is the process of automatically regulating a machine. Not until a feedback function is added does it become automation technology, in the proper sense of the word.

Feedback, by the way, is one of the natural functions of the human body. If I want to pick up a glass, for example, the most direct way of doing so is to move my hand precisely in the direction of the glass. I can do that because my eyes are following my hand movement. If the movement is imperfect, the eyes measure the aberration and transmit it to the brain; then the brain automatically corrects the hand movement so that it can instantly reach the glass. Measuring the aberration and delivering the information to the brain is the process of feedback.

What cybernation involves is the linkage of an automation mechanism with a computer or, to put it another way, with an artificial brain. The result is not merely automatic control, but also the ability to count, remember, and decide — "mental" work on a par with some human feedback capacities.

In developing the coupon vending machine, Omron demonstrated the ability to create cybernation technology completely on its own. That meant that complicated automatic control functions that had previously seemed impossible were brought within our reach. Personally, I felt as if we had been handed a magic wand.

The World's First Unmanned Station

Cybernation was the key to completely automated systems. Starting with control machinery, Omron added feedback functions to produce automation. That allowed the user to realize labor savings brought about by the mechanization of some physical tasks. Then, using computers as artificial brains, we brought about further labor savings by mechanizing some mental tasks. The combined savings of physical and mental work added up to considerable unmanned work. During the decade beginning in 1965, Omron developed three types of revolutionary unmanned systems — unmanned railway station systems, urban traffic control systems, and banking systems.

The coupon vending machine that we had developed for Daimaru remained a complete flop as far as further sales were concerned. Undaunted, I began to look for other uses for the same technology and concluded that there ought to be a similar need among the extensive public and private railroad networks in Japan. Converting our automatic vending technology from food coupons to train tickets was short work, and we then went about selling it. Everyone in Japan knows the results: virtually all of the thousands of railway stations came to be equipped with automatic ticket vending machines.

Remarkable progress was later made in ticket vending technology. Elaborate printing functions were incorporated so that a single machine could automatically print dozens of different tickets. The machines were also provided with the cash-register function of automatically recording the date on which the ticket is issued. Moreover, group control systems were devised, linking sets of a dozen or more vending machines together in such a way that they could recycle coins among one another to make change smoothly.

Then, in 1966, Omron collaborated with the Kintetsu Railway to develop automatic entry and exit gates. The next year, using both automatic vending machines and automatic gates, the Hankyu Railway's Kita Senri Station in Osaka became the world's first large unmanned station.

Areawide Control of Urban Traffic

Omron's involvement in traffic control technology dates from 1963, when we were asked by the Police Science Research Institute to develop a vehicle detector to count the number of cars passing by a given point. As described above, the institute had been associated with Omron the year before, when they asked us for technology to apprehend the "chi-37" counterfeiters.

When we were called in to develop the counterfeit banknote detector, we had never had any previous dealings with the national police force. There was some question as to whether we should accept the commission, because it looked as if the research outlays would be rather high. Personally, I was so outraged by the very idea of counterfeiting, that I was delighted to take on the job. Moreover, as always happens when we are challenged to come up with new technology, my instincts wouldn't allow me to refuse.

We designed the pattern recognition technology that was necessary to verify the genuineness of a banknote within eight days of the original request. The initial test was a great success, and the audience was buzzing about "magic."

With that, we were sure we had produced what was required to solve the case. That thinking was premature, however. To the dismay of the police, not only did the criminals manage to evade capture, but things took a turn for the worse. Having apparently realized that the bills could now be detected, the forgers stopped passing them, and instead used top-quality printing facilities to make a new batch of counterfeit 1,000-yen notes, which were so finely made as to defy imitation. Once again, we had achieved a technological success that seemed to have no commercial potential. Yet this was the technology that led to the development of ticket vending machines, which has become our most successful market division and a major source of revenues.

Furthermore, as a result of our performance on the counterfeit banknote detector, the Police Science Research Institute held a high opinion of the speed, quality, and spirit of service with which we carried out our technical development work. They came back to us the following year, when they wanted to develop a vehicle detector.

In the early 1960s, prevention of traffic accidents and relief of urban traffic congestion were becoming high-priority social issues. By 1967, the government, backed by substantial appropriations from the Diet, had begun to carry out comprehensive three-year and five-year traffic control facilities plans. In 1963, we became involved in the preparatory stage, when it was deemed necessary to develop a traffic signal equipped with a vehicle detector. The existing fixed-interval traffic signals changed with unvarying frequency, whether it was the middle of the rush hour or the dead of night, and the rush-hour traffic jams had become a major headache for the police. It was necessary to redesign the traffic signal system to conform more closely to actual conditions, and for that purpose, reliable readings were needed for traffic density in various directions and locations. This was the impetus for requesting a vehicle detector. We delivered it two months later.

Technically speaking, the vehicle detector was based on the contactless proximity switch that Omron had developed in 1960. The principle of the switch is that when a metal object approaches the sensor coil a current is released, and when it draws away the current is cut. Accordingly, when a coil measuring about two meters (six feet) square is embedded in a roadway, the metallic content of each passing car is sufficient to make the switch send out a pulse. The pulses are tallied electronically, and the result is an accurate traffic count.

The next step was to construct a full-fledged electronic traffic control system by connecting the vehicle detector to such Omron specialties as automatic control devices and computer circuits. We wasted no time in completing that development work. In 1964, working with the local police, we tested the first prototype of our electronic traffic control signal in Kyoto, at one of the city's worst bottlenecks. What we had developed was officially termed the "automatic induction electronic traffic control signal." What it made possible was spot-control of traffic flows.

We progressed to the line-control level in 1965, with a system that covered a dozen intersections along Naniwa Suji through central Osaka. Then, in 1967, we succeeded in implementing area-control of traffic flows, over a matrix covering more than thirty intersections in the Ginza in Tokyo. The wide-area electronic control technology used in the Ginza experiment represented the first true traffic control system.

Vending Machines that Accept Cards

Canteen, the largest American maker of vending machines, asked us in 1964 to work on designing a machine that would accept credit cards. At the time, vending machines for coffee, candy, and the like were in wide use in the United States, and of course they were designed for coins. As credit cards were coming into widespread use, Canteen was thinking about modifying its products accordingly.

My acquaintance with Canteen began in 1963, during my second visit to the United States. I had gone to Chicago to attend a vending machine show, and while there, I visited the head office of Canteen, in the Merchandise Mart, to try to sell them some microswitches. As it turned out, the Canteen models that included microswitches were manufactured by a subcontractor, whom I had been advised to meet.

Nevertheless, I took that occasion to inquire whether Canteen was making high-performance, electronic vending machines. "Not yet," was the answer. I responded, "Why don't I come back next year and show you our high performance electronic model, adapted for U.S. coins?" They seemed to be very interested.

The next year, as promised, we sent a food coupon vending machine that would accept U.S. coins, and Mr. Yamamoto, the director of our Central R & D Laboratory, went to Chicago to present it. The demonstration was a huge success; they could only marvel at our technology. Unfortunately, unlike in Japan, where cafeteria customers view models of the food and pay in advance, Americans were accustomed to selecting their food and then paying for it at the end of the line. In other words, the Omron food coupon vending machine had no prospective market in the United States.

After seeing the demonstration, however, Canteen president Patrick L. O'Malley had an idea. "If you've got the technology to make something like this," he told me, "couldn't you modify it so that a credit card could be used to buy things from a typical vending machine?" At that point there were some four million vending machines in service in the United

States, but all of them were coin-operated, and this was beginning to become a problem. The majority of Americans by then had credit cards, and it seemed that it would soon be possible to eliminate cash in every situation — with the exceptions of tips and vending machines. By president O'Malley's estimation, if vending machines could accept credit cards, then vending machine sales would probably increase by some 30 to 40 percent.

Upon hearing this idea, Mr. Yamamoto instantly remembered the pattern recognition technology that we had developed for the counterfeit banknote detector. After the meeting, he cancelled his other appointments and went back to his hotel. He began putting his ideas on paper, and worked clear through the night drawing up specifications. The next day my third son, Yoshio, who was then working in our New York office and had come to Chicago for the Canteen presentation, translated the rough notes into English and typed them up. On the following day they went back to Canteen.

The top officials of the company gathered to examine the materials and held a brief meeting. "Look," they said afterwards, "we're very interested. We'd like to ask you not to talk to any other company about this. We'll give you whatever cooperation we can, and if you can actually develop it, we'd like to be the sole agent in the United States."

Mr. Yamamoto began the development work immediately after returning home. Starting with the pattern recognition technology from the counterfeit banknote detector, the researchers designed a special credit card suitable for optical recognition, and a card reading mechanism. They installed them in a vending machine obtained from Canteen, ran tests, and carried out the necessary adjustments. A research team made several trips to Canteen's R & D headquarters, where cooperative efforts promoted further progress, and finally an optical reader-type credit card system for vending machines was completed. This system supported the on-the-spot payment habits of the American market, but our technicians kept working on to also perfect new technology for accepting prepaid coupons, in the form of a magnetic reader system.

In a joint press conference, held in July 1965 at the Waldorf Astoria Hotel in New York, president O'Malley and I announced the results of our collaboration. It was attended by some sixty reporters, and the "credit card system for vending machines" was given prominent play on that evening's television news programs, as well as in the morning papers. The next month, various trade journals introduced the system with articles and photographs. Not only was this the first product developed by Omron to be graced with the term "system," it was also the first time the company had received any significant coverage by U.S. media.

Exactly a year later, Canteen set up the first card-operated vending machines on its company premises. Unfortunately, the experiment was soon judged a failure. It simply didn't pay to use a computer — still very costly in those days — to handle transactions for items that cost fifteen or twenty cents. Of course we were very disappointed: it seemed that no matter in which direction we turned in retail technology, we could do nothing but spend huge amounts of money developing things that couldn't be sold. It was only recently, in Japan, that credit card sales through vending machines became a reality, and we were able to market exactly the same system. It took nearly twenty years for the world to catch up with us.

Toward a "Low-Cash" Society

Within only a few years, however, the credit card system for vending machines turned out to be related to a more current social need: the demand for automated bank teller transactions.

At Omron, the first sign of this phenomenon was an order received in 1967 from a finance company that specialized in loans to the middle managers of companies listed on the Tokyo Stock Exchange. They wanted a loan machine. What they had in mind was to issue credit cards that could be inserted into a machine to obtain ¥20,000 in cash (about $60). The loan would be payable in quarterly installments at our annual interest of 30 percent, and when it was fully paid, the credit card would be returned.

We were able to provide such a machine by using the credit card system that we had developed for Canteen. The only significant difference was that when the card was inserted, the machine issued not coupons or goods but paper money. It was installed in Tokyo outside the client's office, so that customers could use it after hours. The location, in the Ginza, was close to both the downtown business district and the entertainment district, where a business person might want some pocket money for a drink or a snack.

Then in October 1969, for the Sumitomo Bank, we developed an off-line cash dispenser that used magnetic cards.

Two years later, in June 1971, we set up a similar cash dispenser with a data link to a central computer at the head office of the Mitsubishi Bank, thereby creating an on-line cash dispensing system. That was the first such system ever to be installed anywhere.

From there, banks all over Japan installed cash dispensers that were linked by central computers into bank-wide networks, ushering in the era of "cash card" convenience for withdrawals.

Next, in 1971, Omron developed on-line systems for making deposits; they were tested in 1973 by the Sumitomo Bank, and full-scale production began in 1975. Later, we combined the deposit and withdrawal functions, and brought out automatic teller machines (ATMs).

We then turned our attention to the process of making change, which was a major cause of the long waiting lines at bank windows. The timesaving, laborsaving change machine, which Omron placed on the market in 1972, was capable of breaking a 10,000-yen bill into 1,000-yen or 500-yen bills or into 100-yen coins, at the customer's choice. This was one more application of pattern recognition technology.

Cash dispensers, ATMs, and change machines — these could be called the sacred trinity of bank automation. Having perfected them, we at Omron set out to develop larger-scale banking systems that would combine those three functions and be linked via telecommunications. You might say that we set out to create a "less-cash" society. That is, having concluded that a truly "cashless" society, in which hard money no longer changes hands, was still a long way off, we set our sights on promoting the intermediate phase.

During the decade that began in 1965, then, Omron pioneered the development of three types of large-scale electronic systems: railroad station systems, traffic control systems, and banking systems. The essential thing about each of them is that they are *informationized* systems. I define informationizing as comprehending social activities systematically and serving those systems through cybernation and communications technology. In that sense, then, through our development efforts of those years, we took the first steps in the task of informationizing the world at large.

PART IV

Organization
Follows Strategy

CHAPTER TEN

Producer System

O MRON initiated the development of the automation market in Japan, starting in 1955. We kept the lead by devising and continually improving various types of control equipment required for automation, such as microswitches, magnet relays, and time relays. As a result, our production and sales expanded very rapidly. A primary feature of this sort of business activity is its tendency toward a multiproduct, small-lot production pattern that makes production management quite difficult. Of course, sales growth is always welcome, but if no means of managing production is devised, the situation soon goes out of control. Recognizing this problem at the start, I devoted much thought to it and hit upon the idea of the Producer System.

The Producer System is a method of expanding production in a completely self-sufficient manner, by creating a series of factories in the form of subsidiary companies, instead of adding new factories to the company proper. In actual business terms, Omron would develop a new control device for use in automation machinery and, when it had been taken to the point of commercial feasibility, would form a new, wholly owned subsidiary company. This new "producer" would build a factory for assembly line manufacture of large quantities of a limited number of products. When the next new type of equipment was developed, the next subsidiary was created to produce it. The series of factories that Omron created in this fashion are called producer factories, or P factories.

With rapid proliferation of products, effective management is difficult if everything is produced in the company's own factories. Administration becomes much simpler when the factories are decentralized as subsidiaries and each one makes just a few products in large quantities. Viewed as a whole, the Omron organization is engaged in multiproduct, small-lot production; yet at each one of the various specialized subsidiaries, the situation is high-quantity production of a small set of products. Such a system increases productivity, which is the aim of the Producer System.

Since each P factory is a separate company, naturally it is completely self-sufficient. The ideal size, based on the limit of efficient administration, is about fifty employees. In fact, after the establishment of each P factory, I used to take personal responsibility for all administrative duties until the personnel count reached about fifty.

To further the goal of self-sufficiency throughout our operations, we also spun off separate companies for sales and for research. The number of companies grew quickly. All of them required skilled managers, but since the parent company had no surplus personnel, we couldn't fill the subsidiaries' needs. Our solution was for Omron, the parent, to act as a centralized administration center, taking care of most of the desk work related to finance, personnel, general affairs, materials procurement, and follow-up service. Since both sales and research and development were being handled by specialized subsidiaries, this left the P-factory managers free to concentrate exclusively on production and labor relations. Thus the work of managing the subsidiaries was split between the decentralized management, which the subsidiary did on its own, and the consolidated administrative services of the parent company, with a proportional relation of about 30 percent decentralized to 70 percent centralized.

Take procurement as an example. Each P factory would send a requisition for its parts and materials supplies to the materials department at Omron, which would order the total amounts required for all of the factories and then distribute them as ordered. Capital procurement and accounts payable were also handled by the parent company. Meanwhile, the separate sales company would take delivery of finished goods from all factories and handle the entire marketing process. With this system, we were often able to place subsidiaries under the supervision of young factory managers. I have found that the relatively simple administration of a production line and workforce can be entrusted to just about any middle-level manager.

Decentralizing Management

The Producer System was a form of management decentralization, and in the Japan of the 1950s this was a novel means of running a company. Decentralized operation means that you are placing trust in people's personalities and abilities. Accordingly, if a company takes as one of its goals the stimulation of individual development, then decentralization becomes an ideal corporate pattern.

To a degree that is unusual among Japanese corporations, Omron strives to motivate all employees to display their individuality and ability to their heart's content. We have consistently given authority to act independently to as many employees as possible. Since burdening people with miscellaneous jobs works at cross-purposes to that goal, it is best to divert some duties to a centralized administration. This leaves everyone free to concentrate on the particular jobs that bring out their creativity. While the concept of decentralized management was popularized in Japan by Professor Peter Drucker's visit in 1959, following which the divisional structure was widely adopted, Omron had taken equivalent measures several years earlier in the form of the Producer System.

The first P factory, Nishikyo Electric Manufacturing Company, was established in 1955 in a building leased from a weaving company in the Nishijin district of Kyoto. Its main products were subminiature pressure switches, utilizing our newly developed microswitch, for use in home water pumps. The following year, we obtained another order for the same type of subminiature pressure switches for the same use, this time from a different maker. It was a period of intense competition in the new field of home appliances, and manufacturers were loathe to purchase their parts from the same suppliers as their competitors. Yet there was no other domestic supplier; they had no choice but to come to Omron. To achieve the required facesaving, I established a second P factory, Rakunan Electric Manufacturing Company, on the south side of Kyoto, to produce pressure switches for the second customer.

During the next few years a series of P factories were set up in and around Kyoto: Sagano Electric and Rakuto Electric in 1957, Yamashiro Electric in 1958, Gojo Electric in 1959, Ogura Electric and Tateisi Electric Kusatsu in 1960, and the Tateisi Electric Mishima in 1961.

We turned in excellent results under the 30 percent decentralized, 70 percent centralized Producer System. Net sales grew tenfold in only five years, from ¥0.12 billion in 1954, just before the system was created, to ¥1.2 billion in 1959. The main reasons for our explosive growth were an early recognition of the automation age and our emphasis on research and development to turn out new control devices one after another. Clearly, however, the management revolution instituted in the form of the Producer System contributed greatly to our growth as well.

I attended Professor Drucker's first seminar in Japan as a member of the Japan Office Efficiency Association, and afterward I showed him the sights of Kyoto. I drafted my second son Nobuo as our interpreter, and it was he who suggested that we invite Professor Drucker to stay at our home; as participants in the Kyoto Homestay Program for foreign tourists, we were accustomed to entertaining foreigners.

After Professor Drucker had arrived and seated himself in our parlor, he asked me how many children I had. "I have five sons and two daughters," I replied.

"Even at home, you are an expert at decentralization," he quipped, for he was aware of my Producer System. That was the point where I really began to like the man. Over the years, we became strong friends.

Decentralizing Administration

By 1962 we had set up a total of eleven Producer System factories. The scale of operations gradually expanded at each factory, with some having grown as large as 200 or 300 employees; a total of 1,700 persons were then employed in the entire Omron organization. When the P factories reached that size, the centralized administrative staff that had been functioning smoothly at the main company began to encounter some problems. For example, the main company received all of the orders from customers, distributing them among the various P factories as appropriate. As the size of that job increased, so did the number of employees in the centralized administration offices. Also, in order to properly assign orders to the various P factories, it was necessary to understand the production situation at each plant, for which purpose detailed reports had to be filed every day by each factory. As a result, more and more people at the P factories were kept busy preparing daily reports. The same problem occurred with materials procurement. Overall, head office administration swelled to the point where productivity suffered noticeably. On the other end, meanwhile, the independent companies that ran the P factories began to express the desire to manage affairs on their own.

Taking all this into account, I made up my mind to institute a broad policy shift away from centralized administration. Beginning with the transfer of senior line managers from the head office to the P factories as managing directors, the existing policy of 30 percent decentralization, 70 percent centralization was reversed to a 70/30 percent relation. Broadly speaking, the P factories were given overall responsibility for research and development, accounting, finance, parts and materials procurement, and personnel. At the same time, we abolished the centralized department that had been managing production in a coordinated fashion, and instead began sending orders directly from the sales company to the P factories. As a result, the daily report load at the P factories was virtually eliminated. Because conversion to the new system seemed likely to lead to order pileups at certain factories and to delay some delivery dates, we left the head office with responsibility for obtaining feedback and carrying out adjustments to relieve any bottlenecks.

We called the new system the Autonomous Producer System. It did not eliminate the main points of the earlier Producer System, but rather strengthened the decentralization by fully developing self-sufficiency. The managing directors who were sent from the head office assumed overall responsibility for management of their P factories, and the factory heads became their assistants. Of course, such areas as policy, funding, taxes, and research and development were left in the hands of the Omron head office, but otherwise the managing directors independently handled the P factory affairs.

After switching to the Autonomous Producer System in September 1962, I became keenly aware that a company is a living organism that is constantly changing. It is crucial that managers remain alert to those changes and quickly carry out appropriate organizational modifications.

CHAPTER ELEVEN

Birth of the
Neo-Producer System

I N 1962, as net sales reached
¥3 billion (about $8.3 million)
and paid-up capital was raised to nearly ¥400 million, Omron
Tateisi Electronics entered a new phase of corporate development. Our shares were listed on the second section of the
Osaka Stock Exchange, and on the Kyoto Stock Exchange. In
1965 we moved up to the first section in Osaka, and then in
1966 we were listed on the first sections of both the Tokyo and
Nagoya markets as well.

The Tokyo listing involved a significant condition. The exchange authorities would not allow our shares to be traded
unless we consolidated our sales company and the Producer
System factories into the main company. As it happened,
problems had arisen recently in connection with a certain electrical manufacturer's handling of profits through its subsidiaries, and the Tokyo exchange was in a highly sensitive
mood concerning the existence of subsidiary firms. In listing
our shares for public trading, our ultimate goal all along had
been to break into the Tokyo market, and therefore, despite
our natural reluctance, we agreed to the exchange authorities'
condition. Gritting our teeth, we merged the P factories into

the main company in 1965. It seemed that the curtain had come down on the Producer System.

The following year, however, we resurrected the Producer System in a different form. Whereas the previous P factories had all been located in and around the city of Kyoto, the new plan called for a series of factories throughout Japan, located in small cities with populations of 30,000 to 50,000. The other new feature was that these were to be joint ventures, with between 10 percent and 40 percent of the capitalization supplied through the participation of local parties. We called this the Neo-Producer (Neo-P) System.

We chose the joint venture pattern because we wanted to share the profits with the local areas. Previously our subsidiary factories had been wholly owned by Omron, and all the profits were being siphoned off by the head office in Kyoto, which was not the best way to build up local good will. This time, we decided to consult with the community from the start and invite their capital participation, so that some of the dividends would go directly to the local area. We hoped that the resulting perception of the factory as a local company would yield the benefits of local cooperation and conciliation.

Another reason for dispersing our production operations to other areas was to resolve our manpower shortage. At that time the labor shortage in Japan was well-established. From the standpoint of Omron management the phenomenon had two main features, one positive and one negative. On the plus side was the prospect of higher sales because of the potential for our automation market to expand. On the minus side was the obvious difficulty in securing our own labor force. It was ironic that a maker of automation equipment should be suffering from a labor shortage, but for rapidly growing Omron, a guaranteed labor supply had become an urgent priority.

If it was difficult to find workers in the cities, bringing them in from the countryside was no easier. To bring in people from the outside, dormitory housing was necessary, and that represented an investment of about one million yen ($3,000) per person. As for food, many of them would not be satisfied unless we brought in the local specialties of their home regions, which could mean considerable delivery and handling charges. It seemed unreasonable to burden ourselves with those sorts of added expenses, and we concluded that the only sound policy was for us to move out to the regions where workers could be found.

The small cities of Japan tend to be located in districts with many farming villages, and labor shortages had not become a serious problem on the local level. When it came to building a factory, the costs for land, construction, and wages were considerably lower. Furthermore, since the Neo-P factories would have local investment, we could expect some assistance from the local investors in hiring staff. Indeed, things progressed just as smoothly as we had anticipated, in hiring and other areas as well.

From the outset, the Neo-Producer System factories were set up for self-sufficient operation with the executive directors taking full responsibility. We assigned personnel from the general-manager level of Omron as the executive directors. For other essential staff we sometimes scouted from within our own ranks, and sometimes hired from the outside. The insiders who went over to the Neo-P companies gave up their status as Omron employees, for people at the Neo-P factories had to approach their jobs with the realization that they would stand or fall with the subsidiary firm. As completely independent companies, the Neo-P factories had virtual autonomy in everything from corporate finance to personnel and wages. They were also free to invite employees to become shareholders in the company.

From 1966, when the first factory was established in Iida, Nagano Prefecture, the Neo-P factories have grown into a vigorous production network of some twenty-three factories, including some sub-subsidiary "mini-P" factories (Figure 13).

Going Local

With warmhearted people and an agreeable climate, Kumamoto Prefecture (where I was born and raised) on the island of Kyushu has always been hospitable to cooperative organizations. Omron has established five Neo-P companies there, beginning with the Yamaga Tateisi Electronics Company in 1971.

Actually, the first advance into Kyushu was the Nohgata Tateisi Electronics Company. The economy of the Chikuho coalmining district had collapsed in the early 1960s with the nationwide shift to oil-fired power generation. A few years later, when the Japanese government was providing various subsidies to resuscitate the region, a man named Okada, who

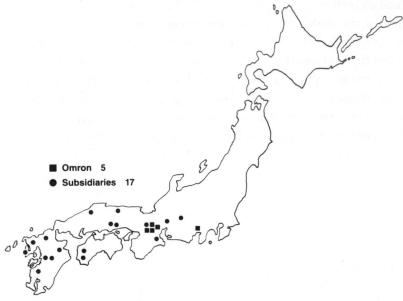

■ Omron 5
● Subsidiaries 17

Figure 13. Neo-P Factories in Japan

had a Christmas decoration company in Kyoto, told me that he had had great success in moving into the Chikuho area. He and I were both members of a group of Sunday painters called the Kyoto Churchill League. We always gossiped as we fooled with our canvases, and that tidbit was one of the rare pieces of business talk that surfaced.

I went as soon as possible to the Fukuoka prefectural offices to inquire about factory sites. They mentioned Nohgata, and I went that very day to the municipal office. I quickly picked out the site on which Nohgata Tateisi Electronics now stands. The price of the forty-one-acre tract, cleared for building, worked out to less than $5,000 an acre. I was delighted. It was perfect for my Neo-P policy. Wanting to start operations there immediately, and since it would take a year or two to clear the land, I rented a recently vacated high school building, and we started making magnet relays there. That was in October 1966. Today the newly built factory specializes in electronic fund transfer systems — electronic cash registers, credit card authorization terminals, and point-of-sale systems.

It wasn't long before the people in the neighboring Kumamoto Prefecture heard about Omron. Sometimes when I visited my home district I was asked to speak to the Business Friendship League, and on one of those occasions an official from Hiratsuka asked me pointedly, "You've come as far as Nohgata. What's wrong with Kumamoto?"

Well, I said, if you had an international airport, or at least a cross-island expressway, if there were some parts manufacturers, then maybe we could do something. Before long, a splendid international airport was indeed built, and the expressway was inching closer. I kept my promise, in 1971 we moved to Yamaga and set up a company.

Who would have thought that the Churchill League, which members regarded as an escape from normal business, would lead to such major business undertakings?

Working with Farmers

At that time, Yamaga was a small agricultural city uncertain about its farming future. A Mr. Miura, chairman of the local agricultural cooperative (the Nokyo) and a member of the prefectural assembly, had conducted surveys and spoken with residents and determined that most of the farming was being done as a sideline. As a result, the city became interested in inviting industrial activity into the region. By moving in and building a factory there, Omron made a substantial contribution toward solving some serious local problems.

Omron appealed to Yamaga as a nonpolluting, high-tech, labor-intensive company. We began by purchasing a building that the Nokyo had been using as a warehouse, and in 1972 we established Yamaga Nokyo Electric Industries. We gathered housewives from the local farming villages who had spare time, and began with the assembly of magnet relays, in cooperation with Yamaga Tateisi.

Development of the company progressed very smoothly. Two years later some 260 housewives were employed there. At the time, the average annual income of a farming household was about ¥500,000 (about $1,600). Each employee of Yamaga Nokyo earned a similar amount. While they preferred not to abandon farming, these agricultural householders were delighted to be able to earn so much money during their extra time. The employees also appeared to enjoy the pleasant work environment. It is difficult to air-condition the old farm houses, and it seems that many of the women were glad to escape the summer heat or winter chill by coming to the air-conditioned factory. The factory also became a social center.

Usually the biggest problem for factories in farming villages is the sudden drastic shortage of labor during the farmer's busy season. Since the Yamaga Nokyo Electric factory belongs in part to the agricultural cooperative, however, workforce schedules can be arranged to insure a steady output regardless of the season. During planting season the workers form groups and do the planting work in shifts, and everyone agrees to stay in the factory for a certain amount of time. These arrangements cover the labor squeeze during the busy seasons. Furthermore, the Nokyo and the company each provide a tractor so that a Nokyo-sponsored youth group can work in the fields, in order to ease the pressures on the housewives who work in the plant.

Thus, we have created a true farm-factory partnership. Omron itself contributed directly to this partnership by building a public clubhouse facility for all sorts of activities, including classes in cooking, flower arrangement, and tea ceremony, as well as for parties. All in all, we have found that the Nokyo Electric format of working with the local agricultural cooperative is a charming way of doing business.

"The Wheelchair Factory"

Another satisfying production partnership is Omron Taiyo Electronics Company, a joint venture with the Taiyo no Ie Foundation (Sun Industries Foundation). This factory is staffed entirely by persons with severe physical handicaps and is often called the "social service factory" or the "wheelchair factory." This is another of our plants on the island of Kyushu, located in the city of Beppu, Oita Prefecture. It opened in 1972.

Every Omron Taiyo employee, including the executive director, is seriously handicapped. The manufacturing subsidiary was set up as a 60/40 joint venture between Omron and Taiyo no Ie. The original capitalization, planned to be five million yen, was reduced by one-tenth in order to give employees the opportunity to buy in. They formed a shareholders association to manage their holdings, and are eligible to hold office in the corporation.

Above all, the creation of this company has allowed handicapped persons to become taxpaying, productive members of society. Here is a prime example of "the company as public service." Moreover, successfully overcoming the risks of creating a "social service factory," which no other large or medium-sized company had been willing to accept, was just the sort of challenge that Omron, with our venture spirit, likes to take on.

The circumstances that led to the birth of Omron Taiyo began one day in 1971, when Dr. Yutaka Nakamura and the literary critic Chieko Akiyama came to see me at the Omron head office in Kyoto, to talk about rehabilitation of the physically handicapped. Dr. Nakamura had gained some fame as an orthopedic surgeon, and in 1965 he established the Taiyo no Ie Foundation at Kamegawa Hot Springs, one of the many therapeutic springs for which the town of Beppu is famous. He personally financed the construction of a building and served as director of the foundation, which was dedicated to providing occupational training to severely handicapped persons. During the first five years, some four hundred people had been trained. Despite persistent efforts to place them in work situations, however, he had only been able to find jobs for about one in ten.

Aware that the most common problem was the difficulty of commuting, Nakamura conceived the idea of a "social service factory" with adjacent dormitories for single and married workers, to eliminate the need for commuting. He crusaded for backing from the national welfare ministry, and finally, in 1971, the government budgeted ¥35 million (about $110,000) for the project.

When they visited me in September, it had not been decided which company would occupy the factory. Dr. Nakamura had approached various parties, big-name corporations as well as middle-sized firms, but no commitment had been forthcoming. Yet if the company were not selected in September and the factory occupied in October, then the special government appropriation would expire. Worried, he cast about for a company that definitely would not let him down. My close friend, Dr. Tomisaburo Hashimoto, suggested Omron. This was the rather desperate message that Dr. Nakamura had for me, and it was a moving story.

At that moment, we were proceeding with the construction of three Neo-P factories, having picked the recession that followed a steep rise in the exchange value of the yen as the right time to move, and we had just finished the necessary recruitment. Dr. Nakamura and I spoke in terms of using ten of those able-bodied employees together with 55 who were severely handicapped, and on that condition, I agreed on the spot to take over the factory. Since an official answer was absolutely necessary by the end of the month, we made all the arrangements on a cash basis, and we completed the formalities at the beginning of October.

On that occasion Dr. Nakamura said to me, "The Taiyo no Ie Foundation never gives the handicapped special consideration, and I hope this company will treat them just as anyone else would be treated." I was more than ready to promise that the new company would stand on its own, like our other Neo-P factories. We placed the Omron Taiyo factory under the administrative supervision of the nearby Nohgata Tateisi Electric Company, as a subcontractor for magnet relays. The conditions were identical to those set for any other subcontractor.

A Profitmaker from the First Year

Omron Taiyo was founded in February 1972 and the opening ceremony was held in April. The three-story building comprised the factory on the ground floor and living facilities for single workers and families on the upper floors. Naturally, the building was fitted for use by the handicapped, with ramps instead of stairways and specially designed toilet facilities. A pre-opening inaugural ceremony, held in Tokyo, was attended by Welfare Minister Sonoda and bureau directors from the welfare and labor ministries. Several speeches were given praising us to the skies for having constructed the first such factory in the world, until I wanted to hide my face in embarrassment.

After beginning operations in April, Omron Taiyo managed to post a monthly surplus of ¥60,000 as early as August. I was amazed; I had expected red ink for the first two or three years. Then, for the first full fiscal year, ending in March 1973, the company showed a profit of ¥1.8 million (about $5,800), and a dividend of 10 percent was distributed.

It should be noted that the wages paid for the subcontracted assembly operations were exactly the same as at other Omron Group subcontractors. Moreover, the percentage of defective products coming off the line was decidedly lower than that of other subcontractors.

There were two reasons for such outstanding performance. In the first place, the employees, who had heretofore been pitied by society as weaklings and denied employment, were finally receiving wages, paying taxes, and even participating in the management as shareholders. Consequently, their work morale at first swelled out of all proportion.

I might add that to this day, most of the severely handicapped people who entered the company at that time still pay taxes. At first, this phenomenon came as a surprise to the Beppu tax office. The new taxpayers themselves were delighted, some of them actually posting their tax payment receipts above the desks in their rooms and folding their hands in prayer. After personally witnessing such a scene, I formed the strong conviction that the handicapped, like everyone else, can find the deepest happiness in the ability to work and earn and lead an independent life.

The other reason for the success stems from Dr. Nakamura's spartan rehabilitation program. One of his rules, for example, was that if someone dropped something from his wheelchair, no one was to pick it up for him. I had raised my own children according to a similar rule: if they fell down and began crying, I would never pick them up and hold them. We have all seen children fall down and begin wailing, only to look around and find nobody there, and then pick themselves up and resume walking naturally. If they are in the habit of being picked up and coddled, then they will take on the character of playing to others' sympathies and relying on them. The handicapped employees of Omron Taiyo Electric Co. have developed self-reliant spirits as a result of Dr. Nakamura's strict regimen. Clearly, those spirits drove the company's fine performance.

CHAPTER TWELVE

Mutsumi-Kai:
The Harmonized Company

*T*HE realization that a business enterprise consists of a social structure as well as a management structure struck me during a management seminar in the mid-1950s. I believe the basic idea originated with Professor Drucker. The management structure forms the system required for the business to achieve its basic purposes. As it hires people to carry out those purposes, a company naturally develops a social structure — a minisociety with a character similar to the larger society within which the company exists. I developed my own name for this internal social structure: *Mutsumi-kai*, which translates as "harmonized group." *Harmony* here means "building respect on the basis of rapport." I announced this name at the corporate anniversary ceremony in 1961. At that time I set out a policy dictating consolidation of company committees concerned with social welfare, pay levels, and service activities, in order to operate with a spirit of "harmony" in keeping with our corporate credo. This single body was to be called the Mutsumi-kai, or Concord Committee.

American companies use a number of techniques to promote human relations within a management structure. In seeking to do the same for the social structure in a Japanese company, I thought it would be a good idea to carefully merge the various activities. I concluded that the Concord Committee should be a democratic mechanism. As the Western saying goes, "Democracy may not be the best system, but it is better than any other."

The Concord Committee represents all Omron employees, management as well as labor. A one-person, one-vote election determines membership, with anyone eligible to stand as a candidate, and the committee selects its own chair. The committee serves to implement the spirit of "harmony" to improve our lives and build a better world. The labor union, too, works toward the goal of "improving our lives," but the union serves a group that excludes the managers and administrators. I reasoned that the Concord Committee, by working to achieve the goal with the cooperation of both management and labor, should surely be twice as successful.

Drawing no distinctions between management and labor, the Concord Committee has monolithic strength. In contrast, the labor union draws the line clearly, and in certain situations the union may even perceive itself as an external body and function accordingly. If such activities reach an extreme, comradeship and goodwill between management and labor may be lost, and the company will cease to function smoothly.

People often think of management and labor as parent and child, but I prefer to think of them as partners in marriage. Husband and wife start out as unrelated strangers, without the blood ties of parent and child, and as the bond between them develops into a relationship of love and mutual trust, the household flourishes in complete harmony. I think of the relationship between management and labor in the same way. All company employees, who came together not out of blood relation but simply through their work situation, share a relationship that resembles marriage. If there is a bond of good feeling and mutual trust between management and labor, the company will flourish, and both sides will prosper, bringing improvement to society as well as to their own lives.

At Omron, labor and management have strong links of good will and mutual trust. I believe that this would not have been possible without the model of the unified Concord Committee. The Mutsumi-kai system was formed to realize an ideal born of my personal inspiration, and I am aware of few comparable examples. In the mid-1960s, however, I happened to attend a seminar in Kyoto at which Professor G. Fischer of the University of Munich, West Germany, propounded his *Partnerschaft* (partnership) theory, and I found it quite similar to my theory of the marriage of management and labor. When I told him about our Mutsumi-kai, he certified it as "the Japanese version of Partnerschaft." Later, through Professor Fischer's introduction, the Mutsumi-kai received feature coverage in a West German management magazine.

I am convinced that the Mutsumi-kai has been a significant factor in the strong growth and development Omron has experienced since the committee was instituted in 1961.

No Contradiction Between Rationalism and Humanism

Management, like engineering, succeeds when it is rational. Rationality, as I understand it, is linked with human respect. Managing a business enterprise on the basis of the principle of self-reliance, which involves deep human respect, is an example of true rationality.

Allowing employees to earn enough, to feel satisfied, and to participate in management is to me the essence of rational management. This is similar to people relying on their own sensibilities to independently maintain their health. It is an extremely humanistic style of management. In short, there is no contradiction between rationalism and humanism. They are complementary aspects of management.

If cost reduction, for example, is the rational objective, the chance of success will be slim without the creation of an environment in which employees can independently tackle the problem. To effect cost reduction in a thorough manner, one usually has to begin the effort during a business slump, when human nature naturally falls in with policy, and employee cooperation is easy to obtain. During boom times, when costs can be cut by obtaining more orders and achieving economies of scale — that is, when extra profit is easily obtained from sales to customers — it will be difficult to motivate people to cut costs inside the company. Once a recession has set in, cutting costs by increasing production becomes more difficult. Everyone can see that the search for profits must begin, in part, with economies in internal management. At such a time, a public relations program highlighting the need for cost reductions should secure full cooperation.

This strategy might seem obvious. Yet, waiting for a recession before implementing economies can be dangerous, because it may then be too late. Realizing that it might be best to act during good times, I took the appropriate steps to achieve as much cost reduction as possible early on.

As a customer-driven enterprise, Omron's responses to the specific demands of its customers often involve serious efforts to cut costs. In addition to a general emphasis on cost-awareness, we implemented a far-reaching economization program in 1965 that achieved impressive results.

We first called in the administrative staff and explained the necessity for cutting costs; then we launched a companywide campaign. A special cost reduction center, consisting of a committee of two people from each division and chaired by the vice president, Takao Tateisi, was established at the head office. To do the job properly, it was essential that the cost reduction committee have complete administrative and operational independence.

The companywide representatives on the committee set a target of ¥140 million ($440,000) to be cut from expenses between October 1965 and March 1966. That figure amöunted to 70 percent of the after-tax profit earned by Omron in the preceding six months — a very ambitious target.

The committee members were left entirely to their own devices, and when the deadline came around in March, the company had achieved cost reductions totalling ¥110 million. During those months, the market for electrolytic copper went through the roof, causing us to spend some ¥18 million more than expected. Otherwise, the total would have been ¥128 million shaved from overall expenses.

The cost reduction committee actually realized 90 percent of its target — a fantastic performance. The total savings of ¥110 million over six months broke down to a ¥48-million reduction in operating expenses, and a ¥62-million reduction in outlays for parts and materials. Seeing no reason to stop, the committee set a target of ¥90 million more for the following six months, ending in September 1966. The actual savings in that period amounted to ¥105 million. The twelve-month total savings was ¥233 million (nearly $750,000).

Obviously, our cost-cutting campaign was a great success. If we had proceeded by simply ordering everyone to shave their budgets, we never could have done so well. Fortunately, we let the employees take charge.

The Omron System of Distributed Results

Omron's unique system of result-based employee dividends was a key factor in the success of our cost-cutting program. Under this formula, the number of months between bonuses is set on the basis of profit and added value. We inserted added value into the formula precisely to link it to cost reductions.

Administrative efficiency is an important element in added value, but as a general rule, most workers, particularly those on the front lines dealing with customers, have little disposition for administration. When it comes to the interest rate on borrowed funds, for example, the executives and financial staff make the decision; people in the field would not be able to handle it. Fluctuations that occur because of economic circumstances have nothing to do with the people in factories or branch offices. Those sorts of fluctuations do cause the profit to rise or fall, but the average worker will be the first to tell you that it is not fair for bonuses to rise and fall accordingly.

Serious cost cutting, though, must include the various expenses for which workers on the line and in the field do have responsibility. For example, executives and division heads can do little by themselves to prevent wasteful use of lights or water. In other words, the rank-and-file employees collectively hold many of the purse strings.

The Omron bonus formula includes added value, defined as the net sales less controllable expenses. Controllable expenses include those for materials, consumable tools, office supplies, packaging, telephone line charges, lighting, heating, and rejected products. Top management cannot effectively control such expenses, even if they make special efforts. The responsibility has to be placed with the general employees. Trimming those costs increases the overall added value, and that comes back in the form of bonuses. Thus, our workers make serious efforts to achieve cost reductions.

High Pay, High Efficiency

"High pay, high efficiency" is one of my management mottos. Please read those words carefully; they are a reversal of the usual philosophy of "high efficiency, high pay."

Garden-variety "high-efficiency, high-pay" thinking, by which wages will be raised if efficiency goes up, is exceedingly obvious to the wage earner. It is not a concept that stimulates outpourings of enthusiasm. Putting it the other way around, as "high pay, high efficiency," means raising wages first and then expecting better performance. That is Omron's way of operating. I am firmly convinced that this improves both morale and productivity.

I first encountered the "high-pay, high-efficiency" doctrine in a book published in England in the 1920s, entitled *The Secret of High Wages*. Five engineers who had gone to America on behalf of the British government had assessed the factors behind the prosperity of American industry after the First World War. Businesses in America, while paying high wages to their workers in order to increase the purchasing power of the citizenry, also had reduced fabrication costs through mass production (known then as "Detroit automation"). Products of uniform standard could be supplied at remarkably low prices. As these vast amounts of products were consumed through the purchasing power that had been supported by a high-wage policy, companies obtained higher incomes and higher profits, allowing them to increase wages further. The secret of American prosperity, the authors concluded, was high wages (Figure 14).

I was a young man when I read that book, and it left an indelible mark on my thinking. "High wages, high efficiency" has always been one of my own secrets of doing business, even though I found it impossible to practice my ideal at first. When the Tateisi Electric Company had fewer than one hundred employees, our wages were substantially lower than those paid by large companies. To the limited extent possible, I gradually made increases, not as rewards for high performance but as stimuli. Finally, we caught up to the salary level of the large companies and by 1965 the Omron pay scale was about 10 percent higher than comparable companies.

Infusing Efficiency

Strictly speaking, our "10-percent-higher" salary scale was 10 percent above the average scales of eighteen companies — the thirteen top Japanese electrical manufacturers, plus the

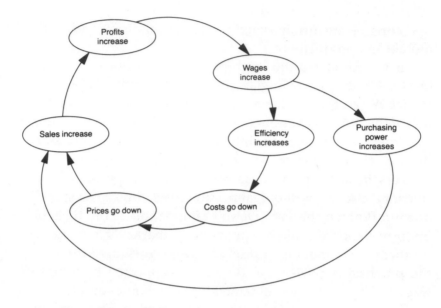

Figure 14. Relationship of High Wages to Profits

five biggest Kyoto-based companies, which were in the category of medium-sized companies. Making salary comparisons meant obtaining data about average age and average compensation, as well as considering such factors as male/female differentiation. In fact, it was not at all easy for us to accurately compare ourselves with those eighteen companies. In 1966, the average age of Omron employees was 23, while that of the other eighteen companies was 27. Since there was no formula available for equalizing average wage data for different age levels, we were forced to devise what might be called the Omron age-conversion formula. Our salaries were broken down into factors such as age, length of service, and education background, which were assigned quantitative values. After the same operations were performed on the data from other companies, meaningful comparisons became possible.

Using the new comparisons, we found that our salary levels were 17 percent higher than the average for the eighteen other companies. At that time, however, Omron employees worked an average of 7 percent longer than those at the other companies. After factoring out that discrepancy, our compensation stood exactly 10 percent higher.

Of course, if salaries are high, then efficiency must also be high, or the company will fall apart. Management cannot afford to express vague expectation of high efficiency. In many cases, pressure must be applied to make high efficiency a reality. In fact, to instill efficiency in others, good managers must themselves be quite efficient.

Basically, salary levels should be set according to degrees of service to the company, on the assumption that when wages are paid according to ability, talented people will be attracted. To introduce an efficiency factor into the pay system, then, salaries should be rationally calculated. Yet, since actual conditions will probably involve various factors related to living standards, it is not so simple after all to inject the merit system into salaries.

Care must be taken to accurately evaluate the levels of ability and service. The proper yardstick is difficult to construct. Having tried out a number of them, I have found that while absolute ratings are always problematic, it is possible to make plausible comparative ratings. The method that I have come to rely on is to first lay out the performance standards clearly and objectively, and then make broad and impartial performance assessments. I should add that as this process is carried out with more and more rigorous impartiality, talented employees will feel the inducement, and the natural result will be the cultivation of stronger capabilities. In contrast, poorly thought out efforts to simply make everybody feel equal will cause talented employees to give up and leave, which is the worst thing that can happen to a company.

Eight Preconditions for Growth

W HAT should be done to set a company on the road to growth? This question has been on my mind for half a century, and in the management of my own company, I have come up with a system. The basic idea is this: If sufficient steps are taken to create the proper conditions, then the company can be more or less left alone, and sustained growth will occur automatically.

The preconditions that should be created are these:

1. A corporate credo
2. Alignment of company goals with instinctive behavior (humane goals)
3. Profit sharing
4. Esprit de corps (and participation in ownership)
5. Policy input from all (self-inclusion)
6. Positioning in growth markets (new products)
7. Original technology
8. Leadership

A Corporate Credo

The first precondition, vital to any company, should be setting a corporate credo. Employees spend the better part of each day at the company, and therefore each must feel that the work has some significance. A companywide understanding of the company's *raison d'etre* makes a big difference to productivity. The Omron motto, devised in 1959 — "At work for a better life, a better world for all." — is a clear, simple expression of Omron's goals, a concise articulation of my business philosophy of the company as a public service.

Alignment of Company Goals with Instinctive Behavior

Secondly, a means must be developed by which people's natural inclinations are linked to the prosperity of the company. Fundamentally, human beings are disposed to act for the perpetuation of the species; this is demonstrated in the tendencies both to avoid situations that endanger one's life and to work in ways that promise a happier future. The company, then, should set goals and carry out policies that will coincide with the urges and actions that employees, as human beings, will naturally exhibit.

An example of this principle in marketing is the production of goods that satisfy the needs of society and more or less sell themselves, as discussed, through the phenomenon known as suction sales. In the same way, when it comes to motivating people, if company policies are aligned with natural human behavior, then without any particular speechifying, the two will work hand in hand. Conversely, if company policy is antithetical to human instinct, then progress will be impossible without the exertion of considerable pressure.

Profit Sharing

The third precondition for growth is a just distribution of profit. Profit is generated by the three elements of capital, labor, and management, and the fruits of their contributions must be divided fairly among the three.

Esprit de Corps and Participation in Ownership

Profit consists not only of cash returns, but also the spiritual dividend of esprit de corps. The creation of a work environment in which such a spirit exists is the fourth precondition. The sense of creative joy that a technician may feel in the research laboratory is one type of distributed profit. Obviously, the best policy is to set up an environment in which the joy of accomplishment can be amply felt. Experience at Omron indicates that today's young generation in Japan is especially unlikely to be satisfied only by their salaries. It would be a mistake to try to attract and motivate people solely on the basis of money. The most effective means for a company to draw out the full power of young employees is to create working conditions that offer them the thrill of creation and the joy of fulfillment.

It is important to strengthen the consciousness of participating in ownership. The feeling that one has a stake in the company is a prerequisite for developing a sense of pride in that company. Having a stake in the company also builds personal pride and increases one's sense of social status.

Policy Input from All

Allowing every employee of the company to have a say in policy is the fifth precondition for growth. Closely connected with esprit de corps, this concept has recently become a more and more important requirement. Substantial changes in management techniques will usually be necessary to give each employee a sense of participation in company policy. This principle of self-inclusion, an idea borrowed from industrial psychology, holds that if you feel personally involved in setting policy goals, then you will follow the program even if there are parts of it that you dislike.

Positioning in Growth Markets

The sixth precondition is positioning in markets with high-growth prospects, an accomplishment requiring quick perception of emerging social needs. This is one of the most important jobs of the executive. If the company is already active in an expanding market, then of course it is good policy to ride out those possibilities. For still greater effectiveness, however, it should break into new markets with high-growth potential. Professor Drucker has emphasized this strategy as key to dynamic, large-scale growth.

Original Technology

Original technology, the seventh precondition for growth, implies strengthened capabilities in research and development. No matter how many strategic high-growth markets a company moves into, it cannot achieve solid development by relying on technical licenses from other companies. There is no getting around the need for technological independence. In cases where outside technology is judged desirable, the company that already possesses a number of its own patents can easily obtain it at an advantage through cross-licensing agreements.

Leadership

Leadership is the final precondition. Even if the other seven elements are all present, they cannot be effectively used if a company lacks the leadership to motivate people. The successful company requires executives and managers who can display outstanding leadership.

All eight of these conditions must be in place in order to make a company grow, but at Omron two of them have proved especially critical to longterm success — *positioning in growth markets* and *original technology*. The other six factors are by now deeply woven into the fabric of Omron's policies. These two require continual reassessment and the ability to shift quickly and learn while in full stride. They will determine the nature and direction of our future growth.

PART V

Toward the Second Era of High Growth

CHAPTER FOURTEEN

Riding the Megatrend

S INCE we pioneered the automation industry in Japan
thirty years ago, Omron has been committed to the venture
spirit, and to tracing our own path. To eradicate the big-business
syndrome that had undermined our venture spirit, I launched
a corporate reorganization program and effected a 70 percent
cure. At present the company is performing well and showing
smooth growth (Figure 15).

From a longer-range perspective, it would seem that Omron
has crossed into its second period of high growth. The first
period was from 1955 to 1970, when our sales totals rose by 30
percent to 35 percent each year. The second period of high
growth, which began in 1983, may well exceed the first, in
terms of both growth rates and continuity.

The leading American social forecaster, John Naisbitt, wrote
in the opening paragraphs of *Megatrends*: "This book is about
ten major transformations taking place right now in our society. None is more subtle, yet more explosive, I think, than
[the] megashift from an industrial to an information society...
I am not, of course, the first to speak about the information society. It is not a new idea. In fact, it is no longer an idea — it is
a reality."

	Net sales	Income before tax	Net Income
1985	293,641	25,882	10,897
1986	277,108	12,438	2,575
1987	278,569	11,417	3,048
1988	315,618	25,798	10,808
1989	not fixed yet		
1990			

Note: Unit = Billion Yen

Figure 15. Omron from 1985 to 1990

The qualitative shift to the information society has already occurred. The industrial revolution in eighteenth-century England, was a motive-power revolution based on the steam engine. It spurred the rapid rise of many industries, including cotton mills, railroads, and steamships. England was able to use this industrial power to take control of the seven seas and enjoy two centuries of enviable prosperity. The information-driven revolution now in progress has strong potential for achieving a scope that rivals the first.

Companies that embark on new roads of activity to ride the megatrend can experience tremendous future growth. On the other hand, companies that remain detached from the trend and continue to operate in the old ways of industrial society will become what are known as structurally depressed industries, and eventually will disappear.

No matter how busy an executive is, his or her most important job is to plot the future direction of the company and to keep the company on course. At this point in history, an executive's first priority is to align the company with the megatrend sweeping us into the information society. Setting a course that ignores this megatrend is like rowing a boat against the current; after a year of toil, you may well find that you have made no progress at all.

3C Technologies Are the Foundation

To jump aboard the megatrend, a company must incorporate the *3C technologies*, which are indispensable to the information society. The three C's stand for computers, communications, and control, the core of high technology. An analogy to the human body reveals the importance of the three C's: computers are the brain; communications, the nervous system; and control, the limbs. Just as the combination of those three organic systems creates the human capability for complex activities, so the union of the 3C technologies allows a company to function in the information society.

The term is based on the phrase "C & C" ("computers and communications"), which came into use in the late 1970s to describe the basic technologies required for the information society. Omron adds the third C, "control," for in our view, brains and nerves are not enough to get the job done. You also need hands and feet — control equipment.

Creating a PC Environment

There is little doubt that companies that continue to rely on industrial-age technology will end up in structural depression. Conversely, those companies in structurally depressed industries which are now crying about slumping business may have a chance of escaping if they make the effort to link up with the 3C technologies. Manufacturers, in particular, without the three C's, will be unable to develop new products to match the needs of the information society.

What about nonmanufacturing companies? Even though they may not need to actually acquire the 3C technologies, they cannot ignore them. As producers begin using the three C's to develop information-related equipment, other types of companies in order to use those products, will have to acquire practical knowledge concerning the 3C technologies.

The most obvious examples are the new media and data processing systems that are in ever wider use, including personal computers, facsimile machines, and word processors. More and more people are being forced to acquire knowledge about the hardware and software of those tools, as if the manufacturers were making a new type of clothing, which the non-manufacturers had to learn how to wear properly.

The remarkable diffusion of personal computers and other data-processing devices during the 1980s shows the extent to which nonmanufacturing companies have introduced the 3C technologies. Supermarkets and delivery services, for example, are revolutionizing their activities by adopting information-handling equipment, and realizing marvelous results. For those who learn to "wear" the three C's well, high growth is possible.

In order to "wear" the three C's, it is necessary to study the basics of hardware and software, and the fastest and simplest way for a company to do that is to create a "PC environment" in which every employee is familiar with personal computers. The first step is to require them all to actually put their hands on the computers. Of course, this applies to manufacturers as much as it does to other types of firms.

At Omron, we set about creating a PC environment in 1981, beginning with the "PC saturation campaign." Over a three-year period we brought one thousand personal computers into operation. Including our affiliates, we have about ten thousand employees, and hence we implanted one PC for every ten or so people. We did not give any orders to "use this PC for this or that purpose." On the contrary, the employees were told that they could use the computers if and when they liked, during work hours or afterward, for whatever purposes they wished, even including private affairs or making up games.

The result: within half a year the employees had developed some three thousand PC programs. Naturally, while some of this software related to their daily work, some of it was purely recreational. The cooking programs developed by some women employees were just one example of the very rich variety. It was because we let them do exactly as they pleased that those three thousand different programs were created. This is precisely what I mean by the term *PC environment*.

Our next step was to begin applying the accumulated software to our business activities. In fact, we decided to go into the consulting business, and we inaugurated this new field of operations in December 1982. As comprehensive office automation consultants, we were prepared to offer advice on software as well as hardware. Besides selling software that had been developed in-house, we also began selling hardware, linking up with twenty-five of the world's leading PC manufacturers as distributor of their products. This branch of operations was provided with its own building, the tenth-floor "My-Com Base Ginza" in downtown Tokyo.

Mastering the Three C's Twenty Years Early

In Omron's case, recognizing the 3C technologies and devising ways to introduce them to the company is not a recent development. We had absorbed two of them by 1965, and we picked up the third shortly thereafter.

To begin with, as a maker of automation equipment, Omron has long possessed the technology of control. Indeed, the contactless proximity switch that we invented in 1959 was the world's first switch incorporating a semiconductor, that is, the first transistorized switch. This was an epochal event in the field of automatic control and a harbinger of the electronics revolution. In 1963, that technology gave birth to our coupon vending machine, which represented a large step forward from contemporary systems in that it was equipped with calculation, memory, and decision-making functions. To make possible such complex functioning, we had combined the automatic control technology that we already possessed — transistorized contactless switches and relays — with computer technology. The application of computers to control equipment is cybernation, and we were proud of our independence in reaching that level of technological strength. At that point we had mastered two of the three C's, control and computers.

The coupon vending technology was later adapted to sell railway tickets, and then we added change-making machines to develop completely automated station systems. But it was the development of traffic control systems that brought Omron into the realm of the third C. First, we invented an induction-type electronic traffic control signal, which connected a vehicle detector to measure traffic and a computer to calculate the best stop-and-go signal timing. We demonstrated it at one of the busiest intersections in Kyoto, then in a series of intersections along a major artery in Osaka. In 1967, we progressed to an areawide control system, feeding traffic through a matrix of more than thirty intersections in Tokyo's frantic Ginza district.

That areawide traffic control system introduced a new element alongside automatic control technology and computer technology. It used communications technology to transmit data collected by vehicle sensors, installed at key points of the traffic matrix, to a central computer, and to send the results of the computer's calculations and analysis to the signals at the various intersections. This incorporation of communications technology meant that by 1967, Omron was equipped with all three of the C technologies, even though nobody was yet talking about the "information revolution" or "3C technologies."

The Deer Hunter Doesn't See the Mountains

Once we had the 3C technologies, we were able to develop several new types of equipment and systems. Banking systems are the prime example. In 1969, Japan's first automatic cash dispensers were installed for a major bank. These were off-line units, not connected by computers. In 1971 we brought out the world's first on-line cash dispenser. Thereafter, Omron continued to set the pace in the diffusion of other types of financial service machinery.

In short, Omron pioneered the development of three types of large-scale systems in the late 1960s and early 1970s: railway station systems, traffic control systems, and banking systems. They share the essential feature of being information-based systems created to meet actual social needs. In fact, at that time the world was just beginning its transformation from the industrial to the information society, and Omron was playing a significant role in that revolution.

To begin commercializing these information-based systems in earnest, we gathered the relevant divisions into a new independent operation wing called Information Systems Headquarters. That was in 1965, before the term "information society" was in general use, but I had picked it up from some specialists who spoke at meetings of a future society to which I belonged.

Naturally, we weren't able to predict the extent to which information systems would infiltrate society, yet we had clearly grasped the general trend, and I feel justified in boasting that we were among the first to begin grappling with the information age. More important, however, is how we did it.

Quite simply, we detected needs for informationized equipment and systems. Since 1955, we had been working steadily to detect the actual needs of society and to develop products that would satisfy them. Automation was our field, but since the automation market did not yet exist, there were no components for use in automation. All of the necessary control equipment was developed by us. If we had not been able to pick up the precise needs for control equipment and to develop the new products through our own efforts, we would have been unable to expand our business.

"Selling products is not enough," was my constant litany to the employees. "I want you to bring back needs from the customers — as many as possible, as quickly as possible. That is the other half of a sales person's job."

By opening up the automation market at a rapid pace, we multiplied net sales tenfold. We held fast to that basic strategy afterwards, as well. One result is that during three decades, Omron has sold some 45,000 different types of control equipment. I know of no other company that has followed the same sales method. Japan is full of companies that search out products developed in Europe and North America, improve on them, pay royalties if necessary, and then produce and sell the new versions. In those cases, the basic product already existed. Those companies do not create products from scratch; they do not add new types of products to the total already available.

Omron searches out needs, not products. When we found a pressing need for a contactless switch, we utilized semiconductors to invent a marketable one. That technology became the foundation for automated station systems, traffic control systems, and banking systems. In the process, we mastered all of the 3C technologies. In retrospect, it is clear that we were developing information-based systems.

We have a saying in Japan, that "The deer hunter doesn't see the mountains." I was so mesmerized by the hunt for deer in the form of the needs of society that I never noticed the mountain of change leading us from the industrial age to the information age. That changes in social needs should move together with changes in the structure of society seems obvious today; as does the observation that as society becomes informationized there will be more work relating to information-based systems. It is no mystery, then, that Omron remains astride the megatrend.

CHAPTER FIFTEEN

A Theory of Historical Innovation

W HEN will the information society begin? When will it end? Those questions took on major importance for Omron during the 1960s, when we were beginning to make substantial investments in information-based systems technology. We needed to know whether the market for such systems could really be expected to grow. To find out, we developed a model for predicting the technological future, called SINIC — Seed-Innovation to Need-Impetus Cycle.

Basically, the SINIC theory presents human history in terms of two cyclic relationships between science, technology, and society. One cycle starts with a major breakthrough in scientific knowledge. This sows the seeds for the development of new technology, which in turn influences society and works as a force for social transformation. The other cycle moves in the opposite direction, beginning with social needs. A crucial need for new technology is eventually satisfied by technical innovation, which in turn induces further scientific evolution. Science, technology, and society, therefore, evolve in cycles, with a change in one realm serving as a cause for or product of the change in another. What fuels this cyclic evolution is the fundamental human desire for continual progress.

Among the innumerable historical events that have occurred since the emergence of our species, the major scientific discoveries make up an exponential curve when plotted in a time series. Such a curve can be used to gauge when a newly developed product will reach its prime, when it will face a period of competition, and when its life cycle will begin to decline. Major historical events coincide with the turning points on this growth curve, making this a plausible tool for extrapolation into the future.

According to the SINIC theory, ten major innovative shifts mark the journey from primitive times to the near future. In prehistoric times society changed from primitive to collective; then came the agricultural and handicraft stages. The next three — industrialization, mechanization, and automation — can collectively be called the industrial society. Finally, we reach the stages of information (cybernation), optimization, and autonomy. The last shift on the SINIC curve ushers in what we envision as a natural society.

The SINIC theory includes an extensive mathematical analysis of those ten stages of society. We began by plotting the growth in economic productivity against the common logarithm of the years to 2033 A.D. This yielded an equation for social progress, from which we derived functions for the process of innovation and for rates of change. The entire theory is outlined in the proceedings of the International Future Research Conference, held in Kyoto in 1970, where I made the first public presentation of the SINIC concept. (*Challenges from the Future*, Vol.2, [Kodansha, Ltd.: Tokyo, 1970]; see appendix for a reprint of portions of this presentation.) (Figure 16)

Forecasting with the SINIC Theory

What transformed society from the age of mechanization to that of automation was automatic control technology, which in turn grew out of the seed of control science. We are now in

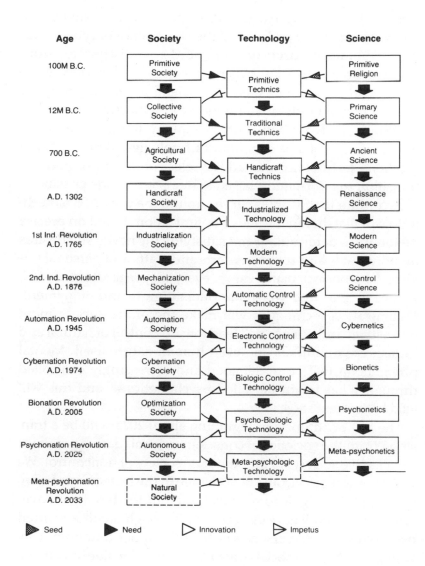

Figure 16. SINIC Diagram of the Ten Social Stages

the information society, the age of cybernation spawned by Norbert Weiner's formulation of the new science of cybernetics. By combining a dozen or more academic disciplines, from mathematics to medicine, cybernetics elucidated human neurological control mechanisms. That scientific seed contributed heavily to the fields of engineering and electronics, and in particular yielded cybernation technology, which is the combination of control and computer technologies. When communications technology was added, electronic control and the transition to information-based systems was made possible.

According to the SINIC curve, around the year 2005 biotechnology will usher in the age of optimization, based on precise methods for determining and satisfying the needs and desires of individuals and society. As arts and crafts and personal services take on increasing value, everyone, regardless of skill, will be able to find work that offers dignity and enjoyment. Optimization techniques will make the entire society more normative, and science will lead toward control of natural and human environments and even human nature itself. Mental phenomena will be understood and increasingly controlled through what might be called psychonetics — and this will lead to the next stage.

The age of autonomy, beginning about 2025, will be a transition from the societies of conscious control (dating way back to collective society) to the "natural" society of noncontrol. We will have adjusted to an era of change in the human condition, in which the struggle for survival and thus for dominance over other humans will have disappeared. Through highly advanced psychology, each person will be able to act autonomously without actualized social controls. Value will reside only in the creation of something new.

The clarification of psychological phenomena will tremendously increase human capabilities, and an even more advanced, utopian society will be sought. The natural society, predicted to begin around 2033, will resemble primitive society, but on a different plane. Wisdom and goodwill will have replaced ignorance and greed as the driving forces of society, and peace, life, and happiness will be of supreme importance.

At present, of course, we are still in the age of cybernation, which the SINIC curve predicts will last from 1974 to 2005. Within that time frame, the job of providing the technology for the age of cybernation can be expected to reach its zenith now. The remaining fifteen years promise to be the golden age of cybernation and information-related activity. Indeed, to run with the main current, companies that have not already done so will have to acquire the 3C technologies rapidly.

On the basis of these projections, Omron should continue enjoying rapid growth for some time.

CHAPTER SIXTEEN

From Selling Components
to Marketing Systems

*I*N 1970, when I created the Information Systems Headquarters, I thought, "We've already entered the information society." During the preceding few years, Omron had fully mastered the 3C technologies and applied them creatively. Integrated systems for railway stations, traffic control, and banking systems had become pillars of the company's operations.

Next we moved into large-scale retailing systems with the development in 1972 of electronic cash registers and point-of-sale (POS) systems. During the 1980s, the transformation from a "low-cash society" to a "cashless society" (which I had anticipated in articles and lectures as early as the 1960s) has come into view. In its corporate reorganization of 1983, Omron combined the retailing and banking systems divisions into the new Electronic Fund Transfer Systems Headquarters. The move anticipated the coalescence of a broad-based market for the coming age of electronic settlement, which would naturally involve still fuller application of the 3C technologies.

In another field, the Tateisi Institute of Life Sciences, a spinoff from the Central Research and Development Laboratory, developed digital electronic sphygmomanometers and thermometers. These proved to be very popular among Japanese consumers, as part of the boom in home health care devices. Recognizing the business opportunities associated with a timeless social need — the universal human desire to live longer with better health — Omron has actively moved forward in the development and commercialization of systems for home health care as well as professional medical treatment.

Meanwhile, in our major Control Systems Headquarters, we took the corporate restructuring of 1983 as an opportunity to shift the operating emphasis from unit sales to systems marketing. The symbol of that strategic conversion was the Omron Technical Fair (OTF), held in the fall of 1983 as part of the celebration of the company's fiftieth anniversary. The OTF brought all of the company's systems and products under one roof, around the theme of "Approaches to Future Technology." After its opening in Tokyo, the fair moved to nine other locations around Japan.

At earlier OTF expositions in 1967, 1970, 1973, and 1978, Omron had displayed the latest capabilities in automation and labor savings, in step with trends in the industrial sector such as factory automation, office automation, and the microelectronics revolution. The OTF had also gained a reputation as a technical information exchange, because seminars were held and visitors were encouraged to participate in various ways. The outstanding characteristic of the 1983 Omron Technical Fair was its shift in emphasis from the display of single products to the display of systems. Reflecting the major product lines and technical directions after the reorganization, the OTF was divided into eight sections: new technology, control components, cybernetic systems, semiconductor production equipment, traffic control systems, electronic fund transfer systems, office automation, and health and medical equipment.

Downstream Markets: Ten Times Larger

The automation-related business that Omron launched in 1955 was basically a unit-sales affair. The business perspective was similar to that held for the mass marketing of items such as beans or sugar or salt. Even now, that is the trend of commerce in general. By 1983, however, Omron was no longer presenting displays of items. Instead, we were showing people the kinds of systems that could be assembled from Omron components, and the types of service such systems could provide. Previously product lines had mainly been commercialized as hardware and exhibited as individual components. Now they were combined in suitable systems, based on software development.

A parallel example from the culinary world might be the marketing of *yakitori*. Chicken and onions, instead of being sold as separate units, are sliced up, placed on a skewer, flavored with a special sauce, and sold as *yakitori*, a product whose value exceeds that of its separate ingredients. The chicken and onion are the hardware, the skewer is the software, and *yakitori* is the system, in this case the product.

When our control components are displayed as separate units, those who are not automation specialists may not understand how they can be used. By contrast, if they are shown in the form of systems, even nonspecialists are immediately likely to think, "We could use something like that," or "If that part were a little different we could probably use this." Besides the systems we had developed earlier for railway stations, traffic control, and banking, a number of applied systems targeted at various industries were also displayed. The reaction was dramatic: During the 1983 OTF we accumulated some twelve thousand inquiry cards from visitors expressing their specific interests or reactions. The majority of those written requests were related to application systems.

In 1984, after analyzing those cards to ascertain actual user needs, we initiated serious marketing efforts for systems and applications. Naturally, we are continuing to market components as separate pieces of hardware, but wherever possible we are working to develop software and market it in combination with hardware. This period was the dawn not only of a new era in Omron sales strategy, but also of an innovative sales method for the Japanese automation components market as a whole.

The annual scale of Japanese automation component production, according to a 1985 survey by the Nippon Electric Control Component Industry Association, is on the order of ¥400 billion (about $2.8 billion), and the greater part of that represents unit sales. Unit sales can be considered to be the upstream market. Accordingly, we can regard sales of modules, assembled components, and the like as the midstream market. Finally, sales of total systems, in which the modules and components are integrated into readily usable packages, constitute the downstream market.

The entire automation market, including the downstream segment, is estimated at more than four trillion yen. That is about ten times the size of the upstream market alone. To move into the downstream market, Omron, which already has a sufficient accumulation of hardware, decided in the early 1980s to strengthen its software development and transfer its marketing emphasis to systems. We are not claiming that it will be possible to move downstream at a single stroke, but we can certainly say at the outset that we have set our sights on something substantial. This is the greatest gain of the 1983 Omron Technical Fair.

Wanted: System Engineers

The biggest obstacle in expanding our marketing activities to application systems is the shortage of system engineers. Under the previous regime of unit-oriented sales, business went smoothly without any system engineers at the sales outlets. But when it comes to selling application systems, qualified engineering support is absolutely necessary. We have sufficient numbers of system engineers in each of our operating divisions for retailing systems, banking systems, office systems, traffic control systems, and so on, but there is no surplus available for assignment to sales outlets. We urgently need to bring in system engineers from outside the company, but we are not the only enterprise in this position. Nowadays all engineers are at a premium in Japan. Even nonmanufacturing concerns, such as trading companies and banks, are recruiting engineers in large numbers. At this point, a half-baked recruiting program has little likelihood of netting able people.

I suspect that the best way to proceed is to establish R & D subsidiaries dedicated to development of application systems at various places around the country, each of them assembling a supervisory staff composed largely of people with local roots. In the past we have found success in this manner, notably through a subsidiary named Tateisi Software, which we set up in Kyoto in 1978 for the purpose of training software engineers. The Omron head office promptly began sending out orders for various types of software, and to fill them the subsidiary had no alternative but to hire additional software engineers. Pressed to the wall, the president of the subsidiary racked his brains for techniques to secure the scarce specialists. Six or seven years later, the company had some 200 software engineers. What is more, Omron never stopped inundating them with orders; in order to handle the deluge, the subsidiary was working with some 50 collaborating enterprises, staffed by about 300 software engineers. Indirectly, then, Omron had procured a total of 500 specialists who were hard at work filling our software needs. Had we set out to hire 500 engineers for our Central Research and Development Laboratory, in all likelihood we could not have assembled the talent. When an independent company is established for a specialized purpose, the results can be amazing.

Software firms are easy to establish, because major equipment is unnecessary. It is simply a matter of setting up shop at various locations. Then, as the head office steadily sends out orders, the head of the new firm is forced to concentrate all available energies on finding talent and setting up collaborations. This is another case in which the "theory of provided conditions" works.

A New Series of Laboratories

Now that we are in the high-tech age, we might as well establish plenty of research facilities. In 1985 we opened the Tateisi Tokyo Telecommunications Laboratory, representing a startup investment of about five billion yen. From an initial 20 or 30 people, the research staff is expected to grow to about 100 by 1990. By then the laboratory should be well into full-scale research in telecommunications and information technology, and as progress is made we anticipate cooperation with the operating divisions on product development. A separate project in the Tokyo area was the establishment of a new software company, which also started with about 30 engineers. In addition, for the last several years we have been establishing research institutes, each staffed with about 30 engineers, at each of the nine "technopolis" research cities in Japan.

The overall plan, conceived in 1985, was to open new R & D centers in ten locations, including Tokyo, beginning with a total of approximately 600 engineers. Because of our experience in securing staff for the new software company in Tokyo, that did not seem to be an unrealistic number. Omron has never found a shortage of fine development engineers who are graduates of regional universities or industrial schools. Also, in recent years more and more young people have been finding urban life unpleasant for various reasons, and making U-turns to return home.

Although we can certainly expect to secure capable staff, we are also aware that some time is necessary to cultivate research skills. Training a software engineer usually requires about a year. System engineers, on the other hand, must have about two years of on-site experience in production and sales sites under their belts, with a total of about three years training required for the well-rounded system engineer to emerge. At this point, such training is one of Omron's largest and most pressing tasks.

The purpose of dispersing our new R & D centers throughout Japan has been to secure system engineers. The Telecommunication Laboratory differs from the other labs in that it lays particular stress on the development of communications technology; this is why it is sited in Tokyo.

Omron has worked steadily and fruitfully in the communications field, including optical telecommunications, ever since its development of traffic control systems in the mid-1960s. In 1983, we completed an optical fiber connection extending more than six kilometers as part of a traffic control system on the Hanshin Expressway between Osaka and Kobe. In 1982, the government of Taiwan gave us an opportunity to fully utilize the latest communications technology, by ordering a traffic control system to cover some 373 kilometers of expressway stretching from Keelung to Kaohsiung. To manage the busiest sections, which ran for 81 kilometers between Keelung and Yangmei and the international airport, optical cable and a private branch exchange (PBX) were utilized; in addition, transmissometers and cable televisions were installed to cope with dense winter fog.

Yet despite its advanced level, Omron's communications capabilities lag behind its technologies of control and computers. As we move into an era of information network systems, we are ever more conscious of the necessity to round out our communications technology. The Tokyo area, which for various reasons is the national center for communications technology, was the only sensible site for our new communications research facility. As the keystone for Omron's mastery of the 3C technologies, the Tateisi Tokyo Telecommunication Laboratory has a vital mission to fulfill.

CHAPTER SEVENTEEN

Aiming for the Optimization Society

T HE conditions outlined in this chapter explain how Omron has already positioned itself on the upward curve of a second era of high growth. We hope that our experience will be a useful example for other companies wishing to ride the megatrend of technological change.

As we approach the 1990s, in addition to completely eliminating big-business syndrome, we are concentrating our efforts on further refinement of the 3C technologies, on the marketing of applications systems, and on the cultivation of the requisite system engineers. I am convinced that when this new management strategy is placed on the right track, Omron's future prospects will brighten considerably.

In conclusion, I will touch on Omron's future with a slightly longer-range perspective. Under the SINIC theory, as described above, the information society began in 1974 and will continue until 2005. At this writing, then, the information society has already run half of its course. Although the next stage of development is not expected to begin for another fifteen years or so, it is now that we should begin preparing for the approaching optimization society.

In the present information society, all sorts of social phenomena are dealt with through the 3C technologies, that is, information-based systems. A basic feature of information systems is that they are largely unmanned, which has led to a dramatic expansion of production capacities, and hence to a materially richer society. At this point, after the first decade of the cybernation society, we have already reached a sufficient level of material satisfaction. The other side of the coin is that major issues of spiritual impoverishment have come to the surface, issues that will fall to the optimization society to resolve. As a Japanese saying has it, "Once fed and clothed, one acquires manners."

To fulfill that vision, it will be necessary to understand and harness the potential of the mind, and our task during the fifteen years remaining in this century is to develop the technology to do so. This is no simple challenge. Research work toward the fifth generation of computers — "thinking computers" — is now under way. Whatever artificial intelligence such computers may have, they will not have true "minds" in the sense of being linked to feelings and spiritual awareness. For that we must await a sixth generation.

Fifth-generation computers will still use silicon chips, but the sixth generation will likely contain biochips as well. The vanguard of biochip research is in the United States, where remarkable results are already being achieved with the aid of military funding. In terms of the SINIC theory, then, the bionation revolution is steadily approaching realization.

At Omron, we believe that it is not feasible to achieve biochip development in a single leap; rather, it should be approached through the intermediate stage of biosensor development. Beginning with biosensor research, Omron is striving to establish the technologies of bionation and lay the groundwork for the optimization society. This is our goal, and it is my conviction that it is also our mission.

Afterword

A Fresh Start for the Holonic Nineties

Reinventing the Company

My father, Kazuma Tateisi, founded Omron in 1933, and all of us in both the family and the company have watched his creation pass first the 50-year mark, then the 55-year mark, with awe as well as satisfaction. Yet ever since I joined the company twenty-odd years ago, I have been very much aware that the Omron of today was really founded in 1955. As my father explains in the early chapters of this book, that was the year he branched into the automation business, not only for his company, but in a real sense for Japan as a whole.

The "second inauguration" of Omron was a bold step into a new and untested market. It was also the beginning of Omron as a truly R & D-driven company. During those early years of market expansion and intense technical progress, Omron adopted the modern management techniques of organization and planning. From 1955, the company set the pace for Japan's high-growth years with steady expansion and regular crossing of new technical horizons. Later, thanks to continuing clear vision, Omron was among the first to recognize big-business syndrome and to shake itself clear of the malady by reorganizing.

Times are still changing, and nowhere more rapidly than in the high-tech control equipment business. The world is edging toward a new humanism that will transform the ways in which we live and work and do business.

I could already sense something building when I became president in 1987. I realized then that it was my job to both support the potential for the coming evolution and stand clear and allow it to be born. For I am convinced that Omron is headed toward a "third inauguration" in the 1990s, possibly at the beginning of the decade.

During the several years leading up to 1955, my father's foresight led him to carefully explore the new concepts of automation and cybernetics. Without knowing quite what to expect, he prepared the company to respond to the first stirrings of the automation market, and thus to ride with the profound changes that we know today as the information revolution.

Likewise, my intuition and training tell me that we are now in a preparatory phase for the humanistic technology of the 21st century.

The landmark opportunity for innovation will appear rather anonymously one day; in the meantime I am doing my best to point Omron in a thoroughly *human* direction. Even as we grow in size and globalize our operations, we are moving across the board to become a customer-driven, employee-oriented company.

Learning from Customers

The changes that we are experiencing in the late 1980s are occurring in two basic directions. One is the maturing of the information society. In market terms, of course, this means that consumers expect more choice, more customized products. Supporting this trend is the rush of "smart" technology into new products and services in everything from cars and electronics to finance and medicine.

The second axis of change today is the emergence of the global society. This is a complex process of integration, with aspects of centralization as well as powerful forces of decentralization. The markets are multiplying even as they are coming together, and communications is taking on new forms and new content as the diverse peoples and needs of the planet increasingly interact with one another.

Where are these changes actually taking place? I think of them as occurring in the lives and jobs of individuals everywhere. This makes it more imperative than ever for the alert company to stay in touch with the daily pulse of human life. Omron has always done its most important business on other people's premises, listening for new needs, learning about the present in order to stay one step into the future. Yet, as a promoter and disseminator of new techniques and equipment, and as a mass producer of thousands of different products, Omron must be careful not to become distracted by its own concepts and activities.

It is now more important than ever to stay in touch with our customers by collecting information, listening to their requests, sensing their next requirements, and constantly finding new ways to deliver value. We are still completing the shift from the "product out" mode of volume production and sales of a few product varieties, to the "market in" mode of providing each customer with maximum amounts of quality, cost, and delivery.

I often tell our employees that learning only from company insiders leads to mere self-satisfaction, and that learning only from competitors leaves us merely tracing the competitor's tracks. This is another way of saying that the basics of true success consist of learning from the customers themselves, and offering products and services that satisfy their desires.

Of course, Omron has long based its activities on the concept of social needs. What has changed is the degree of customer sophistication, and thus the need within Omron for sophisticated response — better information, more quickly, in more places. In fact, the concept of "learning from customers" does not stop with clients; it also includes colleagues within the company and even the people in our private lives. I stress the importance of considering anyone as a customer.

The Ideal Workplace

In the broadest sense, Omron's business operations are aimed more and more at the optimization of human potentials. To me, the most logical way to accomplish this is to put the principle into practice ourselves. We have some fifteen thousand workers in the Omron community worldwide — fifteen thousand challenges in terms of training, motivation, cooperation, satisfaction.

My image of the ideal workplace is a cheerful place that buzzes with activity. I have gone out of my way in the past two years to meet as many employees as possible and to demonstrate firsthand my belief that everyone in the workplace should have a sense of working independently. That means frankly speaking out when she thinks she is right, and it means acting and responding quickly when he sees what needs to be done. Such free and open communication should extend beyond one's own workplace to people in other sections as well. This will strengthen a vital aspect of the job environment: the sense of personal contribution to the workplace as a whole.

A workplace should give off a bright, cheerful ambience to all who visit or work there. The results will be visible in terms of productivity as well as the quality of the employees' lives. Part of the initiative that I hope each employee will exhibit is a desire to contribute to the creation of a cheerful worksite.

The talents of each employee deserve constant attention. The success of any job depends on the worker's basic skills and the application of those skills. For example, many people play golf. I think most of them realize how difficult it is to continue to improve after a certain score has been attained, especially if the basics have not been mastered correctly. My job as president of Omron is no different. If I am not free to develop through continual, independent improvement of my basic skills and their applications, Omron will undoubtedly suffer. The same is true for fifteen thousand others.

By the way, Omron's employment standards were recently modified to do away with the previous emphasis on outstanding scholastic ability. We are actively recruiting similar proportions of other types of people — students who are active in sports, students with strengths in unique fields such as Chinese or astronomy, generalists who are at least moderately strong in many fields. Having come to the conclusion that talent is the key, we have dropped some of our preconceptions about what that talent might be.

Another aspect of the Omron program for revitalizing its human resources is the recently instituted policy of sabbatical leave. I don't know whether I myself will ever be able to take off for a few months at a time in the middle of my career. I am thoroughly convinced, however, that some employees can benefit immensely from paid leave — enough to make it easily worth our salary money in terms of productivity, creativity, and renewal. I might add that sabbaticals were virtually unknown in Japanese commerce and industry when Omron introduced them in 1988.

The Multipolar Company

Just as the conventional image of the employee has changed, so has that of the company that seeks to respond to the world of the 1990s and beyond. A key concept in our present thinking is diversification.

One of the meanings of diversification is moving away from mass production of a few items toward multiproduct manufacturing in small lots. Of course, Omron was a pioneer of this concept, partly because we ourselves design the flexible manufacturing systems that serve this new industrial pattern. As companies in many fields diversify their product lines, the parts and equipment with which we serve them must also diversify. Along with the hardware comes software, which includes a growing body of knowledge in each field about marketing and manufacturing trends.

Up to now, it has been enough for companies to focus on a specific type of activity. Hence manufacturers knew production, trading companies possessed marketing strength, and service companies emphasized their professional specialties. The complexity and interlocking of today's markets, however, are forcing a change in the old pattern. One-dimensional strength is of little use to the customer who needs to understand imports and exports, hardware and software, multiproduct marketing and numerical control.

On the other hand, diversification loses its meaning without a context of integration. At Omron, several things connect the employees who sell switches in Italy with those who inspect medical diagnostic equipment in Japan or develop factory control programs in Chicago. On the purely technological level, the switch, the scanner, and the software could all wind up in the same piece of equipment sooner than you would think, because Omron engineers are constantly on the lookout for synergetic combinations of the company's myriad resources.

Of course, for that to happen, communications would have to be thoroughly integrated. That is also part of the master plan for Omron, and already largely implemented. The philosophical link is also in place, for Omron employees throughout the world and in all fields emphasize product development on the basis of actual or predictable social needs. We encourage them all to be ready for spontaneous, creative communication with customers and colleagues near and far.

The central collection of strategic information from all of our markets is becoming increasingly important as well as increasingly complex. This was the key factor in our decision to establish a second head office, in Tokyo. The capital metropolis continues to grow in size and influence, and its importance to Omron as a market, a recruiting base, and an international financial center have grown apace. While the management functions will remain with our Kyoto head office, Tokyo becomes our key information center.

Omron now views itself as a holonic company. *Holon* is a term derived from the Greek terms *holos*, or whole, and *on*, or particle. Thus holonic refers to a set of holons, or individual components, in close harmony with each other. Another way of viewing the holonic group is as parts that complement each other while also exhibiting individual, semiautonomous functions. In more conventional terms, a holonic enterprise is one in which the separate divisions or functions are synergetically integrated and operated.

The Multilocal Company

Omron has done business on an international scale for several decades, but only now are we beginning to become a truly global company. During the 1980s our sales organizations outside Japan were significantly strengthened, especially with the opening of factories in England, Malaysia, and the United States. In the 1990s, our abilities to serve societies worldwide will take a quantum leap forward.

The multilocal Omron of the 1990s will function through four headquarters, in Japan, North America, Europe, and Asia-Oceania. Each will administer its own, locally sited resources for financing, development, manufacturing, sales, and management. Through our seventy existing subsidiaries and affiliates outside Japan, significant portions of this global net are already in place.

It goes without saying that the multilocal structure will be able to accurately assess and match the regional needs of several continents. In doing so, Omron will be making significant technical, economic, and social contributions to various nations of the world.

The recent appreciation of the yen is not the only factor behind our global strategy. Exports account for less than 20 percent of total company sales as of fiscal year 1988. We have yet to reach our stride in key world markets, and we have decided to expand *within* those markets, through the direct involvement of the multilocal plan.

The basic needs of the 1990s — multipolar diversity and holonic integration — will be generated not only in Japan but also in North America, Europe, and the Asia-Pacific region. To meaningfully serve these requirements, close ties to local markets and societies are increasingly essential. Once again, social needs are the driving force behind our planning.

Omron's most important single asset is the spirit with which we have been inventing the future for several decades. In revitalizing the company for the 1990s, we count renewing and sustaining of that spirit of challenge as our highest goal. As long as the relish for tackling fresh opportunities remains strong, we will find success in the marketplace, in the laboratory, in society, and in our lives.

Here's to a more interesting tomorrow!

Omron's Management Philosophy

1. Four facets of the ideal workplace
   a. A cheerful workplace
   b. A variety of talented workers
   c. Customer satisfaction
   d. Rewards for energy and efforts

2. Three major management attitudes
   a. Learn from our customers
   b. Properly evaluate each employee
   c. Instill a challenging spirit

3. Three major short-term objectives
   a. Re-establish the profit structure
   b. Build the infrastructure for the coming New Society
   c. Revitalize corporate organization

4. Five operations principles
   a. Operations based on mid- or long-term plans
   b. Priority oriented
   c. Real-time operations
   d. Total optimization
   e. An attitude of honesty and modesty

5. "ACTION 61" total innovation activities

Yoshio Tateisi
President
Omron Tateisi Electronics Co.

About the Author

Kazuma Tateisi
1-2 Haruki-cho, Narutaki, Ukyo-ku, Kyoto 616

Personal History:

Sept. 1900   Born in Kumamoto City, Japan

March 1921   Graduated from Kumamoto High School of Technology (present Kumamoto University)

April 1921   Served as an electrical engineer in Hyogo prefectural government

Oct. 1922   Joined Inoue Electric Manufacturing Co., in Kyoto

May 1933   Established Tateisi Electric Manufacturing Co., in Osaka

May 1948   Founded Omron Tateisi Electronics Co., in Kyoto, capitalized with 2 million yen

Oct. 1970   Honored with a doctorate in medical science for research and development of artificial limbs for thalidomide children by Tokushima University, Japan

Nov. 1970   Decorated with the order of the Rising Sun, third class, with star and ribbon from Japanese Government for his contribution to the automation industries with the inventions of precision switches and various control components

June 1987   Retired as Chairman and Representative Director and appointed to Executive Adviser

Official Positions:

Special Director of Kyoto Economists Association
Honorary President of Kyoto Prefectural Employment
   Association for disabled persons

Publications in Japan:

My venture management, Diamond-Time Inc., Japan, 1974
Creation and bringing up, Nippon Economic Journal, 1975
Eternal venture spirit, Diamond Inc., 1985
Revival of entrepreneurial-ship, PHP Inc., 1985
Kazuma Tateisi's management innovation school, Diamond
   Inc., 1988

Special interests:

Painting, YOKYOKU (a "Noh" song), TANKA (Japanese
   poem of 31 syllables), listening to classical music

About the Translator

STEPHEN Suloway has worked in corporate communications in Japan since 1980, and has translated books and articles on Japanese culture. He is an editor of the quarterly *Kyoto Journal*. A graduate of Oberlin College, he was also a journalist in Colorado and Washington, D.C.

Books Available From Productivity Press

Productivity Press publishes and distributes materials on productivity, quality improvement, and employee involvement for business and industry, academia, and the general market. Many products are direct source materials from Japan that have been translated into English for the first time and are available exclusively from Productivity. Supplemental services include conferences, seminars, in-house training programs, and industrial study missions. Send for our free book catalog.

Better Makes Us Best

by John Psarouthakis

A powerful and highly practical guide to performance improvement for any business or individual. Focusing on incremental progress toward clear goals is the key — you become "better" day by day. It's a realistic, personally fulfilling, action-oriented, and dynamic philosophy that has made Psarouthakis's own company a member of the Fortune 500 in just ten years. Let it work for you.
ISBN 0-995 / 1989 / 112 pages / $16.95 / order code BMUB-BK

1992
Strategies for the Single Market

by James W. Dudley

In 1992 the European community will unify to create the second largest market worldwide. Published in England, here is the first comprehensive guide for action for anyone who wants to take advantage of the opportunities, and overcome the threats, that this major changes to the world's economic structure holds. It examines financial structures, marketing programs, political strategies, and much more.
ISBN 1-85091-240-8 / 400 pages / $24.95 / Order code 1992-BK

Inside Corporate Japan
The Art of Fumble-Free Management

by David J. Lu

A major advance in the effort to increase our understanding of Japan, this book shows *why* Japanese businesses are run as they are — and how American companies can put this knowledge to good use. Lu has spent many years in Japan, personally knows many top leaders in industry and government, and writes with a unique bicultural perspective. His very readable book is full of anecdotes, case studies, interviews, and careful scholarship. He paints a well-rounded picture of the underlying dynamics of successful Japanese companies. *Inside Corporate Japan* is a timely and invaluable addition to your library.
ISBN 0-915299-16-X / 278 pages / $24.95 / Order code ICJ-BK

Tough Words for American Industry
by Hajime Karatsu

Let's stop "Japan bashing" and take a good close look at ourselves instead! Here is an analysis of the friction caused by recent trade imbalances between the United States and Japan — from the Japanese point of view. Written by one of Japan's most respected economic spokesmen, this insightful and provocative book outlines the problems and the solutions that Karatsu thinks the U.S. should consider as we face the critical challenge of our economic future. For anyone involved in manufacturing or interested in economic policy, this is a rare opportunity to find out what "the other side" thinks.
ISBN 0-915299-25-9 / 178 pages / $24.95 / Order code TOUGH-BK

Canon Production System
Creative Involvement of the Total Workforce
compiled by the Japan Management Association

A fantastic success story! Canon set a goal to increase productivity by three percent per month — and achieved it! The first book-length case study to show how to combine the most effective Japanese management principles and quality improvement techniques into one overall strategy that improves every area of the company on a continual basis. Shows how the major QC tools are applied in a matrix management model.
ISBN 0-915299-06-2 / 251 pages / $36.95 / Order code CAN-BK

Manager Revolution!
A Guide to Survival in Today's Changing Workplace
by Yoshio Hatakeyama

An extraordinary blueprint for effective management, here is a step-by-step guide to improving your skills, both in everyday performance and in long-term planning. *Manager Revolution!* explores in detail the basics of the Japanese success story and proves that it is readily transferable to other settings. Written by the president of the Japan Management Association and a bestseller in Japan, here is a survival kit for beginning and seasoned managers alike. Each chapter includes case studies, checklists, and self-tests.
ISBN 0-915299-10-0 / 208 pages / $24.95 / MREV-BK

Productivity Press, Inc., Dept. BK, P.O. Box 3007, Cambridge, MA 02140 1-800-274-9911

BOOKS AVAILABLE FROM PRODUCTIVITY PRESS

Buehler, Vernon M. and Y.K. Shetty (eds.). **Competing Through Productivity and Quality**
ISBN 0-915299-43-7 / 1989 / 576 pages / $39.95 / order code COMP

Christopher, William F. **Productivity Measurement Handbook**
ISBN 0-915299-05-4 / 1985 / 680 pages / $137.95 / order code PMH

Ford, Henry. **Today and Tomorrow**
ISBN 0-915299-36-4 / 1988 / 286 pages / $24.95 / order code FORD

Fukuda, Ryuji. **Managerial Engineering: Techniques for Improving Quality and Productivity in the Workplace**
ISBN 0-915299-09-7 / 1984 / 206 pages / $34.95 / order code ME

Hatakeyama, Yoshio. **Manager Revolution! A Guide to Survival in Today's Changing Workplace**
ISBN 0-915299-10-0 / 1985 / 208 pages / $24.95 / order code MREV

Hirano, Hiroyuki. **JIT Factory Revolution: A Pictorial Guide to Factory Design of the Future**
ISBN 0-915299-44-5 / 1989 / 218 pages / $49.95 / order code JITFAC

Japan Human Relations Association (ed.). **The Idea Book: Improvement Through TEI (Total Employee Involvement)**
ISBN 0-915299-22-4 / 1988 / 232 pages / $49.95 / order code IDEA

Japan Management Association (ed.). **Kanban and Just-In-Time at Toyota: Management Begins at the Workplace** (Revised Ed.), Translated by David J. Lu
ISBN 0-915299-48-8 / 1989 / 224 pages / $34.95 / order code KAN

Japan Management Association and Constance E. Dyer. **The Canon Production System: Creative Involvement of the Total Workforce**
ISBN 0-915299-06-2 / 1987 / 251 pages / $36.95 / order code CAN

Karatsu, Hajime. **Tough Words For American Industry**
ISBN 0-915299-25-9 / 1988 / 178 pages / $24.95 / order code TOUGH

Karatsu, Hajime. **TQC Wisdom of Japan: Managing for Total Quality Control**, Translated by David J. Lu
ISBN 0-915299-18-6 / 1988 / 136 pages / $34.95 / order code WISD

Lu, David J. **Inside Corporate Japan: The Art of Fumble-Free Management**
ISBN 0-915299-16-X / 1987 / 278 pages / $24.95 / order code ICJ

Mizuno, Shigeru (ed.). **Management for Quality Improvement: The 7 New QC Tools**
ISBN 0-915299-29-1 / 1988 / 318 pages / $59.95 / order code 7QC

Monden, Yashuhiro and Sakurai, Michiharu. **Japanese Management Accounting: A World Class Approach to Profit Management**
ISBN 0-915299-50-X / 1989 / 512 pages / $49.95 / order code JMACT

Productivity Press, Inc., Dept. BK, P.O. Box 3007, Cambridge, MA 02140 1-800-274-9911

Nakajima, Seiichi. **Introduction to TPM: Total Productive Maintenance**
ISBN 0-915299-23-2 / 1988 / 149 pages / $39.95 / order code ITPM

Nakajima, Seiichi. **TPM Development Program: Implementing Total Productive Maintenance**
ISBN 0-915299-37-2 / 1989 / 528 pages / $85.00 / order code DTPM

Nikkan Kogyo Shimbun, Ltd./ Factory Magazine (ed.). **Poka-yoke: Improving Product Quality by Preventing Defects**
ISBN 0-915299-31-3 / 1989 / 288 pages / $59.95 / order code IPOKA

Ohno, Taiichi. **Toyota Production System: Beyond Large-Scale Production**
ISBN 0-915299-14-3 / 1988 / 163 pages / $39.95 / order code OTPS

Ohno, Taiichi. **Workplace Management**
ISBN 0-915299-19-4 / 1988 / 165 pages / $34.95 / order code WPM

Ohno, Taiichi and Setsuo Mito. **Just-In-Time for Today and Tomorrow**
ISBN 0-915299-20-8 / 1988 / 208 pages / $34.95 / order code OMJIT

Psarouthakis, John. **Better Makes Us Best**
ISBN 0-915299-56-9 / 1989 / 112 pages / $16.95 / order code BMUB

Shingo, Shigeo. **Non-Stock Production: The Shingo System for Continuous Improvement**
ISBN 0-915299-30-5 / 1988 / 480 pages / $75.00 / order code NON

Shingo, Shigeo. **A Revolution In Manufacturing: The SMED System**, Translated by Andrew P. Dillon
ISBN 0-915299-03-8 / 1985 / 383 pages / $65.00 / order code SMED

Shingo, Shigeo. **The Sayings of Shigeo Shingo: Key Strategies for Plant Improvement**, Translated by Andrew P. Dillon
ISBN 0-915299-15-1 / 1987 / 208 pages / $36.95 / order code SAY

Shingo, Shigeo. **A Study of the Toyota Production System from an Industrial Engineering Viewpoint** (Revised Ed.)
ISBN 0-915299-17-8 / 1989 / 352 pages / $39.95 / order code STREV

Shingo, Shigeo. **Zero Quality Control: Source Inspection and the Poka-yoke System**, Translated by Andrew P. Dillon
ISBN 0-915299-07-0 / 1986 / 328 pages / $65.00 / order code ZQC

Shinohara, Isao (ed.). **New Production System: JIT Crossing Industry Boundaries**
ISBN 0-915299-21-6 / 1988 / 224 pages / $34.95 / order code NPS

Sugiyama, Tomō. **The Improvement Book: Creating the Problem-free Workplace**
ISBN 0-915299-47-X / 1989 / 320 pages / $49.95 / order code IB

Tateisi, Kazuma. **The Eternal Venture Spirit: An Executive's Practical Philosophy**
ISBN 0-915299-55-0 / 1989 / 208 pages / $19.95 / order code EVS

Productivity Press, Inc., Dept. BK, P.O. Box 3007, Cambridge, MA 02140 1-800-274-9911

AUDIO-VISUAL PROGRAMS

Japan Management Association. **Total Productive Maintenance: Maximizing Productivity and Quality**
ISBN 0-915299-46-1 / 167 slides / 1989 / $749.00 / order code STPM
ISBN 0-915299-49-6 / 2 videos / 1989 / $749.00 / order code VTPM

Shingo, Shigeo. **The SMED System**, Translated by Andrew P. Dillon
ISBN 0-915299-11-9 / 181 slides / 1986 / $749.00 / order code S5
SBN 0-915299-27-5 / 2 videos / 1987 / $749.00 / order code V5

Shingo, Shigeo. **The Poka-yoke System**, Translated by Andrew P. Dillon
ISBN 0-915299-13-5 / 235 slides / 1987 / $749.00 / order code S6
ISBN 0-915299-28-3 / 2 videos / 1987 / $749.00 / order code V6

TO ORDER: Write, phone, or fax Productivity Press, Dept. BK, P.O. Box 3007, Cambridge, MA 02140, phone 1-800-274-9911, fax 617-868- 3524. Send check or charge to your credit card (American Express, Visa, Master-Card accepted).

U.S. ORDERS: Add $4 shipping for first book, $2 each additional. CT residents add 7.5% and MA residents 5% sales tax.

FOREIGN ORDERS: Payment must be made in U.S. dollars (checks must be drawn on U.S. banks). For Canadian orders, add $10 shipping for first book, $2 each additional. For orders to other countries write, phone, or fax for quote and indicate shipping method desired.

NOTE: Prices subject to change without notice.

UTAH STATE UNIVERSITY PARTNERS PROGRAM

Shigeo Shingo Prize for
Manufacturing Excellence

announces the

**Shigeo Shingo Prizes for
Manufacturing Excellence**

*Awarded for Manufacturing
Excellence Based on the
Work of Shigeo Shingo*

*for North American Businesses,
Students and Faculty*

ELIGIBILITY

Businesses: Applications are due in late January. They should detail the quality and productivity improvements achieved through Shingo's manufacturing methods and similar techniques. Letters of intent are required by mid-November of the previous year.

Students: Applicants from accredited schools must apply by letter before November 15, indicating what research is planned. Papers must be received by early March.

Faculty: Applicants from accredited schools must apply by letter before November 15, indicating the scope of papers planned, and submit papers by the following March.

CRITERIA

Businesses: Quality and productivity improvements achieved by using Shingo's Scientific Thinking Mechanism (STM) and his methods, such as Single-Minute-Exchange of Die (SMED), Poka-yoke (defect prevention), Just-In-Time (JIT), and Non-Stock Production (NSP), or similar techniques.

Students: Creative research on quality and productivity improvements through the use and extension of Shingo's STM and his manufacturing methods: SMED, NSP, and Poka-yoke.

Faculty: Papers publishable in professional journals based on empirical, conceptual or theoretical applications and extensions of Shingo's manufacturing methods for quality and productivity improvements: SMED, Poka-yoke, JIT, and NSP.

PRIZES

Awards will be presented by Shigeo Shingo at Utah State University's annual Partners Productivity Seminar, held in April in Logan, Utah.

Five graduate and five undergraduate student awards of $2,000, $1,500, and $1,000 to first, second, and third place winners, respectively, and $500 to fourth and fifth place winners.

Three faculty awards of $3,000, $2,000 and $1,000, respectively.

Six Shigeo Shingo Medallions to the top three large and small business winners.

SHINGO PRIZE COMMITTEE

Committee members representing prestigious business, professional, academic and governmental organizations worldwide will evaluate the applications and select winners, assisted by a technical examining board.

Application forms and contest information may be obtained from the Shingo Prize Committee, College of Business, UMC 3521, Utah State University, Logan, UT, 84322, 801-750-2281. All English language books by Dr. Shingo can be purchased from the publisher, Productivity Press, P.O. Box 3007, Cambridge, MA 02140: call 1-800-274-9911 or 617-497-5146.

Japan's "Dean of Quality Consultants"

Dr. Shigeo Shingo is, quite simply, the world's leading expert on improving the manufacturing process. Known as "Dr. Improvement" in Japan, he is the originator of the Single-Minute Exchange of Die (SMED) concept and the Poka-yoke defect prevention system and one of the developers of the Just-In-Time production system that helped make Toyota the most productive automobile manufacturer in the world. His work now helps hundreds of other companies worldwide save billions of dollars in manufacturing costs annually.

The most sought-after consultant in Japan, Dr. Shingo has trained more than 10,000 people in 100 companies. He established and is President of Japan's highly-regarded Institute of Management Improvement and is the author of numerous books, including *Revolution in Manufacturing: The SMED System* and *Zero Quality Control: Source Inspection and the Poka-yoke System*. His newest book, *Non-Stock Production*, concentrates on expanding U.S. manufacturers' understanding of stockless production.

Dr. Shingo's genius is his understanding of exactly why products are manufactured the way they are, and then transforming that understanding into a workable system for low-cost, high-quality production. In the history of international manufacturing, Shingo stands alongside such pioneers as Robert Fulton, Henry Ford, Frederick Taylor, and Douglas McGregor as one of the key figures in the quest for improvement.

His world-famous SMED system is known as "The Heart of Just-In-Time Manufacturing" for (1) reducing set-up time from hours to minutes; (2) cutting lead time from months to days; (3) slashing work-in-progress inventory by up to 90%; (4) involving employees in team problem solving; (5) 99% improvement in quality; and (6) 70% reduction in floor space.

*Shigeo Shingo has been called the father of the second
great revolution in manufacturing.*
— Quality Control Digest

The money-saving, profit-making ideas... set forth by Shingo could do much to help U.S. manufacturers reduce set-up time, improve quality and boost productivity ... all for very little cash.
Tooling & Production Magazine

When Americans think about quality today, they often think of Japan. But when the Japanese think of quality, they are likely to think of Shigeo Shingo,... architect of Toyota's now famous production system.
Boardroom Report

Shingo's visit to our plant was significant in making breakthroughs in productivity we previously thought impossible. The benefits... are more far-reaching than I ever anticipated.
Gifford M. Brown, Plant Mgr.
Ford Motor Company